A Visitor's

The Battles of Arras South

Bullecourt, Monchy-le-Preux, Wancourt and the Valley of the Scarpe

The statue of the Digger in the Memorial Park at Bullecourt is by sculptor Peter Corlett. It is a replica of his father, Private Kenneth Corlett, who served at Bullecourt with 4/Australian Field Ambulance.

A VISITOR'S GUIDE

THE BATTLES OF ARRAS SOUTH

Bullecourt, Monchy-le-Preux, Wancourt and the Valley of the Scarpe

Jon Cooksey & Jerry Murland

Pen & Sword
MILITARY

An imprint of
Pen & Sword Books Ltd
Yorkshire – Philadelphia

First published in Great Britain in 2019 by
PEN & SWORD MILITARY
An imprint of
Pen & Sword Books Ltd
Yorkshire – Philadelphia

ISBN 978 1 52674 239 1

A CIP catalogue record for this book is available from the British
Library

Typeset in Ehrhardt by
Mac Style
Printed and bound in the UK by CPI Group (UK) Ltd,
Croydon, CR0 4YY

Pen & Sword Books Ltd incorporates the Imprints of Aviation,
Atlas, Family History, Fiction, Maritime, Military, Discovery,
Politics, History, Archaeology, Select, Wharncliffe Local History,
Wharncliffe True Crime, Military Classics, Wharncliffe Transport,
Leo Cooper, The Praetorian Press, Remember When, White Owl,
Seaforth Publishing and Frontline Publishing.

For a complete list of Pen & Sword titles please contact
PEN & SWORD BOOKS LTD
47 Church Street, Barnsley, South Yorkshire, S70 2AS, England
E-mail: enquiries@pen-and-sword.co.uk
Website: www.pen-and-sword.co.uk

Or

PEN & SWORD BOOKS
1950 Lawrence Rd, Havertown, PA 19083, USA
E-mail: Uspen-and-sword@casematepublishers.com
Website: www.penandswordbooks.com

CONTENTS

INTRODUCTION AND ACKNOWLEDGEMENTS

A Visitor's Guide to the Battles of Arras – South is the seventh in a series of guidebooks in which we have designed routes to provide the battlefield tourist with the opportunity to appreciate and explore the more remote parts of the Western Front. Most historians agree that Arras, and the almost continuous fighting that took place around it, made it one of the key battlegrounds on the Western Front. Yet even after the centenary of the Battle of Arras in April and May 1917 it still fails to attract the same volume of visitors which are drawn to Ypres to the north or the Somme to the south. To an extent this is understandable; the gradual residential, commercial and industrial development of Arras has inexorably encroached on many of the

Ordnance found near Bullecourt in the summer of 2017 awaiting collection by the French Département du Déminage.

battlefield sites that were once familiar to soldiers from both sides of the wire, yet despite this, there is still a great deal to see in what was an absolutely vital sector of the Allied front.

Where possible we have used quiet roads and local pathways but please be aware that speeding traffic and farm machinery is always a possibility, even on the quietest of roads. Whilst we have ensured that vehicles are not left in isolated spots, we do recommend you take the usual precautions when leaving a vehicle unattended by placing valuables securely in the boot or out of sight and, being northern France, it is always advisable to carry a set of waterproofs and have a sensible pair of boots or shoes to walk in. Within the built-up areas cafes and refreshment stops are usually open during normal hours but it is a good idea to take something to eat and drink when away from your vehicle for any length of time. Cyclists will recognize the need to use multi-terrain tyres on their bikes and require the use of a sturdier hybrid or off-road machine. Regular visitors to the battlefields will be familiar with the collection of old shells and other explosive material that is often placed by the roadside by farmers. By all means look and take photographs but please do not touch as much of it is still in an unstable condition.

The historical information provided with each route has of necessity been limited but we have given an overview around which to develop your understanding of what took place and why. Nevertheless, we have made some suggestions for further reading which should widen your appreciation of the events that took place on this sector of the Western Front over 100 years ago. Visitors to the German cemeteries at Neuville-St-Vaast and St-Laurent-Blangy will appreciate the section covering equivalent ranks, as will those visiting the French National Cemeteries at Notre-Dame de Lorette and La Targette. Those of you who wish to find the last resting place of the soldier poets and writers or the Victoria Cross winners will find the relevant section in the appendices of some use.

In acknowledging the assistance of others we must once again express our gratitude to Trevor Harvey, Sebastian Laudan for his wonderful help with researching German accounts of the battles, Peter Oldham for his advice on various pill-boxes in the area and Nigel Cave for his assistance with maps of the underground cavities that lie hidden beneath the Arras landscape.

VISITING MILITARY CEMETERIES

The concept of the **Imperial War Graves Commission (IWGC)** was created by **Major Fabian Ware** (1869–1949), the volunteer leader of a Red Cross mobile unit which saw service on the Western Front for most of the period of the war. Concern for the identification and burial of the dead led Ware to begin lobbying for an organization devoted to burial and maintenance of the graves of those who had been killed or died in the service of their country. On 21 May 1917 the Prince of Wales became the president of the IWGC with Fabian Ware as its vice-chairman. Forty-three years later the IWGC became the **Commonwealth War**

Fabian Ware was the first vice-chairman of the IWGC.

Graves Commission (CWGC). Neither a soldier nor a politician, Ware was later honoured with a knighthood and held the honorary rank of major general. The commission was responsible for introducing the standardized headstone which would bring equality in death regardless of rank, race or creed and it is this familiar white headstone that you will see now in CWGC cemeteries all over the world. CWGC cemeteries are usually well signposted with the familiar green and white direction indicators and where there is a CWGC plot within a communal cemetery, such as **Camblain l'Abbé Communal Cemetery**, the familiar green

The headstone marking the grave of Private Charles Mossery at Bois-Carre British Cemetery is of a standard pattern which you will find on all First and Second World War graves. Post-war CWGC headstones have a notch in either shoulder.

A profusion of CWGC signposts in Héninel.

and white sign at the entrance, with the words *Tombes de Guerre du Commonwealth* will indicate their presence. The tall Cross of Sacrifice with the bronze Crusader's sword can be found in many cemeteries, where there are relatively large numbers of dead. The larger cemeteries, such as **Wancourt British Cemetery**, also have the rectangular shaped Stone of Remembrance. A visitor's book and register of casualties is usually kept in a bronze box by the entrance. Sadly, a number of registers have been stolen and to prevent this from happening you may find a cemetery register in the local *Mairie*.

CWGC cemeteries are noted for their high standards of horticultural excellence and the image of rows of headstones set amidst grass pathways and flowering shrubs is one every battlefield visitor takes away with them. On each headstone is the badge of the regiment or corps or, in the case of Commonwealth forces, the national emblem. Below that is the name and rank of the individual and the date on which they died together with any decoration they may have received. Where the headstone marks the grave of a non-Christian, the

Tombes de Guerre du Commonwealth

Commonwealth War Graves

CWGC burials in communal cemeteries are marked by a green and white sign containing the words Tombes de Guerre du Commonwealth *at the entrance.*

emblem most commonly associated with their faith replaces the simple cross. Headstones of Victoria Cross winners have the motif of the decoration inscribed on it. At the base of the headstone is often an inscription chosen by the family. Headstones marking the unidentified bear the inscriptions chosen by Rudyard Kipling, 'A Soldier of the Great War' or 'Known unto God'. Special memorials are erected to casualties known to be buried in the cemetery but whose precise location is uncertain.

French War Graves

There are two French national cemeteries in the area covered by this guidebook, the *Nécropole Nationale de Notre-Dame de Lorette* and the *Nécropole Nationale Neuville-St-Vaast, 'La Targette'* on the D938, but the visitor will find the concrete white grave markers used by the French *Ministère de la Défense et des Anciens Combattants* in a number of CWGC cemeteries and plots. French military cemeteries are usually marked by the French national flag and those which are contained within communal cemeteries are often indicated by a sign

French war graves within communal cemeteries are marked with a distinctive blue and white sign at the entrance.

at the cemetery entrance bearing the words: *Carre Militaire, Tombes de Soldats, Morts pour la France.*

German Cemeteries

The German War Graves Commission – *Volksbund Deutsche Kriegsgräberfürsorge* – is responsible for the maintenance and upkeep of German war graves in Europe and North Africa. As with CWGC cemeteries, these are clearly signposted with a black and white sign bearing the words *Deutscher soldatenfriedhof*. Visitors to the German

German cemeteries are signposted with a black and white sign bearing the words Deutscher soldatenfriedhof.

cemetery north of Neuville-St-Vaast and that at St-Laurent-Blangy, will find them both in stark contrast to CWGC cemeteries. They still exude a dark and often sombre ambiance exacerbated by the dark metal and stone grave markers bearing the name, rank, date of death and occasionally the unit. Like many French cemeteries, they contain mass graves for the unidentified and headstones with up to three or four names on each one.

Equivalent Ranks

We have produced a rough guide to equivalent ranks which should assist you when visiting the cemeteries and memorials referred to in the guidebook.

British	German	French
Field Marshal	Generalfeldmarschall	Maréchal de France
General	Generaloberst	Général d'Armée
Lieutenant General	General der Infanterie/Artillerie/ Kavallerie	Général de Corps Armée
Major General	Generalmajor	Général de Division
Brigadier General	No equivalent rank	Général de Brigade
Colonel	Oberst	Colonel
Lieutenant Colonel	Oberstleutnant	Lieutenant Colonel
Major	Major	Commandant/Major
Captain	Hauptmann/Rittmeister	Capitaine
Lieutenant	Oberleutnant	Lieutenant
Second Lieutenant	Leutnant	Sous Lieutenant
Warrant Officer	Feldwebelleutnant	Adjutant
Sergeant Major	Offizierstellvertreter	Sergent Major
Sergeant	Vize-Feldwebel	Sergent
Corporal	Unteroffizer/Oberjäger	Caporal
Lance Corporal	Gefreiter/Obergefreiter	No equivalent rank
Private, Trooper, Sapper	Schütze/Grenadier/Jäger/ Musketier/Infanterist/Garde/ Soldat/Pionier/Fahrer/Füsilier Kanonier/Dragoner/Husar/ Kürassier/Ulan	Soldat/ Chasseur/ Artilleur/ Légionnaire

HISTORICAL CONTEXT

By 9 October 1914 the French Tenth Army, under the command of Général Louis Maud'huy, had managed to prevent a German occupation of Arras. To the north, the French had been pushed west from the Douai Plain, up and over the Vimy Ridge and off the heights of the Notre-Dame de Lorette spur. Neither side appeared to have the resources to encircle the other and, as the so-called 'race to the sea' ran off north and into Belgium, German attentions focussed on Ypres and the Yser. All hopes of a Christmas victory for the *Kaiser* were dashed by the spirited Belgian defence of the flooded land north of Ypres. The desperate fighting around

Général Louis Maud'huy in conversation with two of his men.

the city itself in October and early November 1914 finally ended any hope of a 1914 German breakthrough to the Channel ports.

The First Battle of Artois, 17 December 1914–13 January 1915

With the French commander-in-chief, Général Joseph Joffre, as its architect, Général Paul Maistre's XXI Corps attacked the northern and western outskirts of Carency in an attempt to seize the heights of Notre-Dame de Lorette. Simultaneous attacks by Général Henri-Phillipe Petain's XXXIII Corps were pitted against the Berthonval Ridge and the north eastern outskirts of Arras by Général Gilbert Desforges' X Corps. They were a disastrous failure, with the French reporting casualties of some 30,000 killed, wounded and missing. In April 1915

Général Joseph Joffre was the French Commander-in-Chief until December 1916.

Général Victor d'Urbal replaced Général Louis de Maud'huy as commander of the Tenth Army.

The Second Battle of Artois, 9 May–18 June 1915

Carried out with British co-operation further north at **Aubers Ridge**, the initial French attack ruptured the German line and captured Vimy Ridge but reserve units were not able to reinforce the troops before German counter-attacks forced the French back, about half-way to their original jumping-off point. The British attack at Aubers Ridge (9 May 1915) was another costly failure and further offensive action was suspended until 15 May. Despite the setbacks, however, the French offensive had advanced the front line towards Vimy Ridge and established a significant foothold on the Notre-Dame de Lorette plateau. (The 1915 British battles, including the Battle of Loos, are covered in our visitor's guide to *The Battles of French Flanders*.) On 12 May 1915 Carency was taken and Ablain-St-Nazaire fell soon afterwards. Neuville-St-Vaast was captured on 9 June and the German-held 'Labyrinth' trench complex fell eight days later. However, the cost in French casualties alone has been estimated at over 100,000, a figure that becomes even more staggering if the 27,684 British casualties are added.

The Third Battle of Artois, 25 September–11 October 1915

This offensive was conceived on the premise that the Allies would deliver simultaneous blows against the shoulders of the German-held Noyon Salient; the French hitting the Champagne sector and the Notre-Dame de Lorette spur with the British striking further north at Loos. The French XXXIII Corps took the Château de Carleul and Souchez and cleared the eastern slopes of Notre-Dame de Lorette; the crest of Vimy Ridge was again reached with French units reporting they were amongst the orchards of La Folie Farm. Once again the attack stalled in the face of powerful German counter-attacks and the French suffered another 50,000 casualties. **Loos**, the third British failure of the year, concluded with 50,000 casualties and the resignation of the British commander-

Sir Douglas Haig.

in-chief, **Sir John French**, who was replaced by **Sir Douglas Haig**. A number of historians have written off the Artois offensives as an expensive French blood-letting that achieved little but, in the authors' opinion, the continual French attacks in Artois not only squeezed the Germans into a tighter perimeter on Vimy Ridge, but facilitated the Canadian Corps' success in April 1917.

Lieutenant General Sir Julian Byng.

On 1 March 1916 the British XVII Corps, commanded by **Lieutenant General Sir Julian Byng**, took over the Vimy Sector and **Lieutenant General Sir Edmund Allenby's** Third Army began moving into position along the line east of Arras, facilitating the French Tenth Army's move to Verdun. The British occupancy of the Vimy Ridge sector was characterized by almost continuous mining operations that turned the front line into a maze of mine craters and resulted in the German attack of 21 May 1916 which drove the British 47th Division off the crest of the ridge and back towards Zouave Valley. A British counter-attack was prevented by Haig, who, at that time, was more than preoccupied with planning for the British offensive on the Somme which began on 1 July 1916. Three months later the Canadian Corps, now under the command of Julian Byng, was assigned to the Vimy Sector.

Lieutenant General Sir Edmund Allenby.

In December 1916, Joffre was replaced as French commander-in-chief by **Général Robert Nivelle**, who promised a new combined Allied offensive on the Aisne and at Arras. Charmed by Nivelle's rhetoric, **David Lloyd George**, the British Prime Minister, made little secret of his support for Nivelle and his distaste for the conduct of British operations on the

Robert Nivelle, the architect of the 1917 offensive.

Western Front. Thus, by the spring of 1917 Arras had become the focus of the next major British offensive, albeit with the British playing a supporting role to the main French assault on the Aisne.

The Hindenburg Line

In late 1916, Royal Flying Corps (RFC) aviators reported the construction of a new double trench system being dug some distance behind the existing front line. Running from Arras to Soissons in the south, it was known as the *Siegfried Stellung* by the Germans and the Hindenburg Line by the British, and would shorten the German front line by some 40km. From Tilloy-lès-Mofflaines the Hindenburg Line ran southeast behind Neuville-Vitasse and down into the valley of the River Cojeul, before crossing the river between St-Martin-sur-Cojeul and Héninel and climbing Henin Hill. Curving to the east, it continued towards Fontaine-lès-Croisilles, dipping into the Sensée Valley to the west of Fontaine before ascending once again, this time onto the high ground known as 'The Hump', before it enveloped Bullecourt.

The order to retire behind the Hindenburg Line – codenamed *Alberich*, after the dwarf in Wagner's series of epic musical dramas *The Nibelung Ring Cycle* – was given on 4 February 1917. *Alberich* was to be preceded by five weeks of total devastation of the area to be evacuated; a scorched earth policy designed to deny the British the use of buildings or land and although it was not applauded by all German commanders, it allowed the Germans to withdraw effectively under the very noses of their enemy. The German retreat to the Hindenburg Line is officially recognized as occurring between 14 March and 5 April 1917, during which time there were a number of British actions against German outpost garrisons at Écoust-St-Mein, Croisilles and Hénin-sur-Cojeul. The British attack by the Third Army at Arras was confined to the northern sector of the Hindenburg Line where the zones of defence were still relatively incomplete, but further south they presented an altogether more difficult proposition.

The Arras Offensive, 9–14 April 1917

Due to the scope of this guide we have not been able to describe the subsidiary attacks on Fresnoy and Arleux-en-Gohelle. The opening attacks of the Arras Offensive can be divided into two battles; **Lieutenant General Sir Henry Horne's** First Army assault on Vimy Ridge and the **First Battle of the Scarpe**, involving Lieutenant General Edmund Allenby's Third Army, in which the First Army took Vimy Ridge and the Third Army took most of their objectives, including Monchy-le-Preux and the Wancourt Ridge.

Battle of Vimy Ridge, 9–14 April 1917	
I Corps: Lieutenant General Arthur Holland	24th Division
Canadian Corps: Lieutenant General Sir Julian Byng	1st–4th Canadian Infantry divisions

First Battle of the Scarpe, 9–14 April 1917	
XVII Corps: Lieutenant General Sir Charles Fergusson	4th, 9th, 34th and 51st divisions
VI Corps: Lieutenant General Sir Aylmer Haldane	3rd, 12th, 15th, 17th, 29th and 37th divisions
VII Corps: Lieutenant General Thomas D'Oyly Snow	14th, 21st, 30th, 50th and 56th divisions
XIII Corps: Lieutenant General Sir Walter Congreve	2nd Division
Cavalry Corps: Lieutenant General Sir Charles Kavanagh	1st–3rd Cavalry divisions

On 16 April Nivelle launched the **Second Battle of the Aisne** along the Chemin des Dames which was intended to break through the German lines and link up with the British in the north. It failed miserably and completely altered the rationale of the Arras offensive, forcing Haig to refocus his thinking. Thus, the **Second Battle of the Scarpe** was fought between 23 and 24 April, involving one division from the First Army and ten from the Third Army. Apart from the 63rd (Royal Naval) Division (RND) taking Gavrelle in the First Army Sector, the largely under strength Third Army made little progress, despite the 15th Division taking Guémappe.

Lieutenant General Sir Henry Horne.

Bullecourt

The two attacks on Bullecourt were the preserve of Sir Hubert Gough's Fifth Army and the 1st ANZAC Corps. The first attempt was a total failure but the second managed to breach the Hindenburg Line and take the village.

Lieutenant General William Birdwood.

First Attack on Bullecourt, 11 April 1917	
V Corps: Lieutenant General Sir Edward Fanshawe	62nd (West Riding) Division
1 ANZAC Corps: Lieutenant General William Birdwood	4th Australian Division
Second Attack on Bullecourt, 3–17 May 1917	
V Corps: Lieutenant General Sir Edward Fanshawe	7th, 58th and 62nd divisions
1 ANZAC Corps: Lieutenant General William Birdwood	1st, 2nd and 5th Australian divisions

The Third Battle of the Scarpe

The battle began on 3 May and involved fourteen divisions along a 26km front and was designed to coincide with the second attack on Bullecourt. Unable to advance in the face of German resistance, the ill-fated and mostly unnecessary offensive was called off the next day. The Battle of Arras officially ended on 17 May, although a limited attack at Roeux on 5 June regained the remaining ground lost on 15/16 May, and it was here the line stabilized for the remainder of 1917.

The German Spring Offensive, 1918

On 21 March 1918 Operation *Michael* was launched from the Hindenburg Line in the vicinity of St-Quentin with the objective of breaking the Allied line. In the face of overwhelming German forces the British Fifth Army fell back in disarray. Much of the ground fought over was the residual wilderness of the Somme offensive in

1916 and was named the **First Battle of the Somme 1918** by the British Battles Nomenclature Committee, the French preferring to call it the *Second Battle of Picardy*. On 28 March 1918 the focus of the German attack switched to the British Third Army around Arras. Operation *Mars* was intended to breach the British defences north and south of the Scarpe, take Arras and secure the high ground of Vimy Ridge but, by this stage, the men on the ground knew what to expect and the German Seventeenth Army floundered against strong, well-organized defensive positions. By 5.00pm the offensive had ground to a halt on both sides of the Scarpe, with appalling German casualties. Nowhere had the German spearhead penetrated more than 2 miles and Arras remained firmly in British and Commonwealth hands leaving the Germans with few territorial gains.

The Advance to Victory
On 26 August 1918 the British First Army widened the attack on the Germans with the Second Battle of Arras of 1918, which included the Battle of the Scarpe 1918 and the Battle of the Drocourt–Quéant Line (the German *Wotan Stellung*) on 2 September. The war had finally left Arras and the surrounding area behind as it moved east.

VISITING THE AREA

Visitors to the area can either stay in Arras or take advantage of the profusion of bed and breakfast and self-catering establishments in the area. If you are intending to base yourself in Arras the four-star **Hotel Mercure** near the railway station, which is situated on the Boulevard Carnot, offers the advantage of an underground car park. There are numerous other hotels in the city. The **Holiday Inn Express** on the Rue du Dr Brassart is also near the railway station, whilst the three-star **Hotel Ibis Arras Centre les Places** is in the heart of the city on the Rue de Justice. A little further out the **Ace Hotel** on the D60 at Beaurains is located near Telegraph Hill and offers good, no frills value with a restaurant/grill a short walk away. For those of you who wish for a more outdoor experience *Camping la Paille Haute*, at Boiry Notre Dame, is just over 6 miles from Arras and offers mobile homes to rent and has a heated swimming pool.

Using this Guidebook
The Arras area is characterized by its rolling hills and valleys and whilst walkers should have little difficulty, bikers will need a decent hybrid or off-road machine equipped with suitable tyres as some of the tracks we describe can become muddy after periods of wet weather. In compiling the guide we have taken the liberty of using a number of abbreviations in the text. With German units we have simply trimmed Infantry Regiment and Reserve Infantry Regiment to IR and RIR. Thus Infantry Regiment No. 73 becomes IR 73, Reserve Infantry Regiment No. 165 becomes RIR 165 and Fusilier-Regiment 90 becomes FR 90. British battalions and units have also been abbreviated, for example – the 4th Battalion Bedfordshire Regiment becoming 4/Bedfords. Where we refer to casualties the number quoted is usually taken from the battalion's war diary and includes officers and men who were killed, wounded or missing after the engagement.

Number	Route	Distance	🚶	🚲	🚗
1	Feuchy Redoubt	1.6km / 1.0 mile	✔		
2	Battery Valley and Observatory Ridge	4.9km / 3.0 miles	✔	✔	
3	Roeux	3.0km / 1.8 miles	✔	✔	✔
4	Telegraph Hill and The Harp	5.9km / 3.6 miles	✔	✔	
5	Monchy-le-Preux	4.5km / 2.8 miles	✔	✔	
6	Wancourt	8.8km / 5.4 miles	✔	✔	
7	Bullecourt	7.3km / 4.5 miles	✔	✔	
8	Southern Car Tour	43.5km / 27 miles		✔	✔

To assist you in your choice of route we have provided a summary of all eight routes in the guidebook together with an indication as to their suitability for walkers, cyclists or car tourists. Distances are in km – the first figure in the table – and miles and to assist you in finding the starting point for each route we have provided the co-ordinates. The circular alpha/numeric references in the text of each route correspond directly with those on the relevant map. We hope you enjoy exploring the Arras battlefields as much as we have.

Route 1

Feuchy Redoubt

Coordinates: 50°17'43.18" N – 2°50'01.50" E
Distance: 1.6km/1.0 mile
Grade: Easy (total ascent 23m)
Suitable for: ╫
Maps: Série Bleue 2406E – Arras

General description and context: This short route can be combined
with **Route 2** and is inextricably linked with the events at 'Railway
Triangle' east of Arras and what tank pioneer Frank Mitchell MC
called the 'Bank Holiday cruise' of a single Mark II Tank – No. 788
named *Lusitania* – of 9 Company, C Battalion, commanded by **Second
Lieutenant Charles Weber**. Weber's tank – one of two assigned to
the 15th Division – was to assist with the clearing of the Triangle –
Geleisedreieck on German maps – and was then to advance beyond
Feuchy to the Wancourt–Feuchy Line.

Weber arrived near his start point by 4.00am but was delayed
when he discovered that the 'bolts connecting plate on back axle to
extension shaft were found to be missing'. It took another 5½ hours to
find spares and fix the problem before *Lusitania* clattered into action
at 9.30am. He caught up with the infantry 'just in front of the Blue
Line', just under halfway between Railway Triangle and the bridge
at **Spider Corner**, 150m or so southwest of the **Feuchy Redoubt**. It
was just as well, as by then the attacking force of 44 Brigade of the
15th Division was held up by heavy machine-gun fire directed from
the railway embankments further on. Informed that the infantry
needed his assistance, Weber mounted the Arras–Douai railway line
and instructed his driver to drive east:

> Fired two rounds of 6-pounder at machine gun in wood north
> of Railway [Watery Wood, now gone and area covered in
> factories] ... Heard no more from this gun ... [after a halt to
> fill with petrol] proceeded towards Blue Line. Half way over
> Sgt Latham informed me that all Infantry were following,
> they arrived [at Helle Trench] almost simultaneously with us,

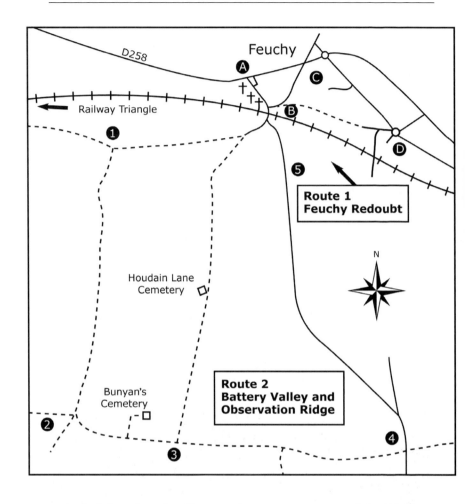

in fact too close to allow me to use my guns, and found the Germans with their hands up. Proceeded straight along railway to FEUCHY REDOUBT, firing on same with 6-pounders and Lewis guns.

For the men of the 15th Division that morning, Weber's appearance must have seemed like Divine intervention and we join *Lusitania's* journey at Spider Corner from where we walk up the track leading to site of the former Feuchy Redoubt. Finally, after a visit to Feuchy British Cemetery, we conclude with a short walk back to the communal cemetery via Chemin des Fonds.

Directions to start: Feuchy can best be reached via the D258 from St-Laurent-Blangy. Park outside the communal cemetery. **Ⓐ**

Route description:
With the cemetery on the right continue for 150m to the railway arch. After *Lusitania's* gunners had fired on the garrison of Feuchy Redoubt – the high ground over your left shoulder – Charles Weber saw Germans 'evacuate this work, half running to the rear and half to dugouts close to Railway Arch'. This is the site of that railway arch at a point called Spider Corner on British trench maps. Looking at the maps it is not difficult to see why this spot got its name, the six 'legs' of roads and rail lines emanating from one point – the railway bridge – resemble a large arachnid.

Imagine now half the German garrison running towards you from site of the Feuchy Redoubt on your left to take cover in dugouts in the embankment here. Weber edged *Lusitania* forward:

> Went on and inspected this arch, firing on same with 6-pounders at anything resembling a machine-gun emplacement. Found we were now under our own barrage and were being shelled by an anti-tank gun. Went back up slope to see what had become of our infantry, found them on top … Turned and proceeded towards arch again. Observed an infantry signal from a party which had

The metal barrier at the start of the uphill walk to the Feuchy Redoubt.

come up along the railway line and got to the arch. Sat outside the arch while this party took the Germans prisoners.

After inspecting the arch at Spider Corner, retrace your route and take the rising grass track which you can see on the right. ❸ This may be the slope Weber refers to in his account of the battle but he is rather vague on detail and could well have regained the railway via another route.

Go through the metal barrier – there is a sign on the barrier restricting access to traffic other than pedestrians – and continue uphill with embankments to either side. After 400m stop. The numerous tentacles of the Feuchy Redoubt trenches – some maps have it as the 'Feuchy Work' – smothered the knoll to your left in the triangle made by the Chemin des Fonds and the Rue d'Athies. ❸ The ground is now partly covered by residential and commercial buildings.

The track now descends to meet **Rue du Petit Bois** which runs parallel with the railway line. After passing a wooded area on the right you will come to **Rue Bertholeux** on the right which leads up to the level crossing. Again, this could be the sunken road described by Weber where *Lusitania* broke down whilst trying to cross the railway line. Weber's movements after leaving Spider Corner are detailed in the C Battalion Narrative of Operations: 'The tank then left the

The track takes the visitor through woodland before arriving at a level crossing on the right.

railway embankment and attacked 400 yards along a sunken lane, it attempted to exit the lane and cross the railway embankment but broke down with magneto trouble; stopping for half-an-hour to let the engine cool down. The magneto was repaired, the bank was crossed.'

Weber had to abandon his 'car' *Lusitania* at 9.30pm that night after the magneto finally 'gave out' and although his crew salvaged the machine guns, it was eventually destroyed by a direct hit from a British battery the following day. Weber received the MC for his actions whilst his sergeant, F. Latham, received the MM.

Continue to the roundabout where you will see a CWGC signpost directing you to **Feuchy British Cemetery ⓓ** on the right. We describe the cemetery and the actions in and around the village in **Route 8**.

Return to the roundabout and bear left, following signposts for *la Cimetière* on the D258. This is **Rue d'Athies** which runs along the northwestern edge of the Feuchy Redoubt. After a further 240m you will pass a road on the left leading to the housing estate we saw earlier in the walk. The Feuchy Redoubt is now on your left as you continue down to the roundabout. At the roundabout the **Rue de Fampoux** joins from the right and it was along this road that a German light railway ran, connecting the front line east of Arras with Fampoux and the back areas. Turn left at the roundabout and take the next road on the left – Chemin des Fonds – which will take you back to the railway arch and ⓐ the communal cemetery. As you make your way back to your vehicle reflect on the memories of Captain Philip Christison of 6/Cameron Highlanders who was somewhere near here in the village at around 6.00pm on 9 April 1917:

> we all advanced rapidly and by 1800 hours had captured the strong Feuchy Redoubt and the village. I was re-organising … when an extraordinary episode happened. A mounted officer in the uniform of the Essex Yeomanry galloped into the village shouting 'Get out quick, retire. The Germans are on you in great numbers, you have no chance.' One of my subalterns, Donald Ross, a Canadian, at once shot him dead and we found he was a German officer in disguise from his papers.

Walking along the road note how high the ground is to your left and how the Feuchy Redoubt would have dominated the area. The sharp-eyed amongst you will notice the large concrete block in the field to the right which was part of the original German fortifications.

Route 2

Battery Valley and Observation Ridge

Coordinates: 50°17′43.18″ N – 2°50′01.50″ E
Distance: 4.9km/3.0 miles
Grade: Moderate (total ascent 43m)
Suitable for:
Maps: Série Bleue 2406E – Arras

General description and context: The route for this walk is contained within the combined map for **Route 1** and **Route 2** found on p. 12 and can easily be combined with **Route 1**. Observation Ridge was defended by the Prussian IR 54 and IR 51 which had concentrated the men of their companies into deeply entrenched and heavily wired 'islands of resistance', each hosting a machine gun whose field of fire interlocked with that of its near neighbours some 200–300m distant. It was a formidable line and protected the field guns of the 11th Infantry Division dug into earthworks in **Battery Valley**. If the strongpoints on Observation Ridge fell then the logical corollary was that the guns in Battery Valley would also be taken.

The British attack was spearheaded by the 15th (Scottish) Division in the north and the 12th (Eastern) Division in the south. The 15th Division ran into difficulties at **Railway Triangle**, where Lieutenant Charles Weber's tank, *Lusitania*, shifted the advantage and led the Scots along the line of the Arras–Douai railway to Feuchy. The 12th Division advanced up the slope from Arras towards **Observation Ridge** and eventually outflanked the numerous strongpoints and by 10.50am 8/Royal Fusiliers (36 Brigade) were digging in on their objective at **Houdain Lane Trench**. The credit for capturing the guns in Battery Valley fell to 5/Royal Berkshires (35 Brigade) who passed through the Fusiliers to take the crest of Observation Ridge before the surviving men ran down the slopes into Battery Valley. Assisted by 10/Scottish Rifles and 7/8 Scottish Borderers from the 15th Division, the German gunners were routed and the British finally subdued those who for so long had made their lives a misery in the trenches in front of Arras.

The communal cemetery at Feuchy offers plenty of parking.

Directions to start: Feuchy can best be reached via the D258 from St-Laurent-Blangy. Park outside the communal cemetery as for **Route 1**.

Route description: From the car park **Ⓐ** by the communal cemetery – the same starting point for **Route 1** – follow the road to the railway bridge at **Spider Corner**. Pass under the bridge and turn right along the track – **Chemin de Feuchy** – which runs parallel to the railway embankment. Go straight on – past the turning for Houdain Lane

The railway bridge at Spider Corner.

The track leading uphill from Spider Corner to Observation Ridge.

Cemetery – and continue uphill. At the time of writing this section of the track proved to be rather an untidy part of the route as it was obviously being used regularly by fly-tippers dumping large piles of rubbish. Do not be put off by this, however, as the track eventually leaves the refuse behind on its way to the start of Observation Ridge and the views across to Arras make it clear why this was such an important tactical feature for the Germans to hold. At the top of the hill, after some 550m, is a turning to the left ❶ whilst ahead is the track that continues to **Railway Triangle**.

Turn left along the track – **Chemin de la Cour au Bois**. You will now travel parallel to the German Helle Trench which ran just to the left of the track. This was roughly the 'Blue Line', the second main objective for the British in the attack of 9 April 1917. Continue and stop after 200m. You have just passed through the site of what were at least three belts of heavy barbed wire entanglements and are now standing on what was the German north-facing **Feuchy Switch Line** which crossed the path from right to left and ran almost all the way back to Spider Corner. About 400m to your right – towards the industrial buildings – was the **Hart Work** island strongpoint and 200m further on again – on the site now covered by the industrial area – was the line of Hermies and Heilly trenches, which made up a section of the initial objectives – the 'Black Line' – of the 15th Division.

Captain Douglas Cuddeford's 12/Highland Light Infantry was one of the support battalions of 46 Brigade, following up the two assaulting brigades and eventually he was ordered forward:

We pushed on to the main support trench of the enemy front defences, a thickly wired trench named on our maps Hermes [*sic*] Trench ... the enemy support trench was a very deep one, much deeper than any ... we had seen on the Somme ... It was badly damaged by our artillery preparation ... as was evident by the number of dead and wounded Germans lying about ... I remember one young German soldier there who had been disembowelled by a shell splinter. He was lying on the fire step with his intestines looped up in a bag formed by his undershirt pulled over them, and as we moved about in the trench he eyed us with an air of mild interest, as if we were the first British soldiers he had ever seen.

Continue up the track and note that in a further 350m **Houdain Lane Trench** came in from the left before running along the track for another 50m before cutting west at right angles to meet the German

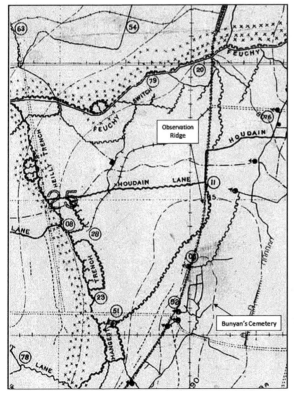

A trench map illustrating the German defensive positions west of Observation Ridge. The approximate position of Bunyan's Cemetery is also marked.

third line position near the Heron Work strongpoint to your right. This island of resistance was one of several, strung like beads along the line of the German third main position running south to Tilloy-lès-Mofflaines, almost parallel to the industrial area you can see to your right: Hamel Work was a little north of Heron Work with Holt Work and Hotte Work further south respectively. It was here that the German machine-gunners inflicted heavy casualties on the attacking battalions. **Private Alf Razzell**, serving with 8/Royal Fusiliers, remembered his company being held up by a machine gun: 'He was positioned in a shallow trench and was traversing his gun in a 180 degree arch. In short rushes, as the traverse passed us by, we gradually formed a semi-circle around him until he was in rifle grenade distance. Inevitably, he and the gun were silenced.'

As the track continues to climb up Observation Ridge it is worth considering the account written by *Leutnant* **Schlensog** of IR 51 who stubbornly maintained that the reason the strongpoints were overwhelmed was because they ran out of ammunition, 'as soon as we stopped firing we were overrun by the enemy'. Schlensog's evidence may have contained an element of truth, but to all intents and purposes the strongpoints were outflanked.

Across to the left you should be able to see the Cross of Sacrifice of **Houdain Lane Cemetery** and a little further still beyond that the Cross of Sacrifice of **Bunyan's Cemetery** comes into view. Continue to the crosstracks and stop. The track straight ahead leads to Tilloy-lès-Mofflaines, but it was some 250m along the track to the right – at **Hangest Trench, ❷** which crossed it, running north–south – that Norfolk-born, pre-war railway porter and builder **Sergeant Harry Cator**, serving with 7/East Surreys, was awarded the Victoria Cross on 9 April 1917. Already a recipient of the MM for bringing in thirty-six wounded men from no-man's land on the Somme in 1916, Harry Cator's platoon was suffering heavy casualties from a German machine gun in the vicinity of Hangest Trench. Under heavy fire

Sergeant Harry Cator earned his VC at Hangest Trench.

Cator and another man broke cover and attacked the gun and when his comrade was killed Cator charged on alone – scooping up a Lewis gun and ammunition pans on his way – and succeeded in reaching the German trench. On spotting another machine gun, he killed its crew and an officer and held the trench to such effect that bombers, following up, were able to capture 100 prisoners and five more machine guns. Wounded by a shell fire five days later, Harry Cator recovered and went on to serve as a captain in the Home Guard during the Second World War and was commandant of a POW camp. He retired from the army in December 1947 and died in Norwich in April 1966.

We are now going to take the left-hand track, which bends round to the left following the CWGC signpost to **Bunyan's Cemetery**. The cemetery is another 260m further along the track on the left and is reached by following the grass track.

Bunyan's Cemetery
With the exception of 19-year-old **Private Thomas Ferrier** (A.6) of 1/Royal Scots Fusiliers, the remaining infantry burials are all from the 12th Division and all from the opening day of the Arras offensive. There are seven men from 7/Norfolks buried here, all casualties of their advance north of the present-day D939. **Private John Talbot** (A.13), aged 22, of 7/Norfolks enlisted in December 1911 and was one of twenty-four Norfolks casualties incurred on 9 April, only half of whom have a known grave. His brother, Robert, survived the war. If you are looking for a grave on which to place a

Bunyan's Cemetery.

cross of remembrance then look no further than 21-year-old **Private Albert Huckle** (A.3), who was another Norfolk Regiment soldier who hailed from Wellingborough in Northamptonshire. A former apprentice, he was one of three children born to Sarah Huckle. His name also appears amongst the 676 names on the Wellingborough War Memorial.

Apart from the infantry there are thirty-eight men from the 12th Division's artillery, who began their advance at 11.30am in support of the infantry and were killed mainly during counter-battery work later in the offensive. Such was the case with 21-year-old **Gunner Clarence Smith** (D.9), who served with C Battery, 62 Brigade and was killed on 3 June, and 21-year-old **Gunner Percy Lunn** (D.7) of A Battery, 62 Brigade, who was killed at Tilloy-lès-Mofflaines on 8 June. Two officers who were killed on 18 April 1917 were **Second Lieutenant Robert de Mussenden Leathes** (B1) and **Lieutenant Harold Hughes-Gibb** (B2), who were both serving in B Battery, 62 Brigade, Royal Artillery.

Retrace your route to the main track and turn left to follow it gently downhill to another track on the left ❸ and stop. **Houdain Lane Cemetery** is 600m further up this track and although not on our route, is easily accessed from this point. However, if you are considering visiting the cemetery by car the track is not suitable for vehicles with low ground clearance.

Houdain Lane Cemetery
This is another isolated battlefield cemetery with nine unidentified casualties amongst the seventy-six burials. There are thirteen men from 13/Royal Fusiliers who were killed on 9 April with two more who probably died of wounds a few days later. The Fusiliers were from the 37th Division and, having lost direction, drifted too far south and became embroiled in the 12th Division's fight for Battery Valley; some even penetrated as far as Orange Hill and dug in on the northern side, facing Monchy-le-Preux. The youngest of these is 17-year-old **Lance Sergeant William Wolstenholme** (H.2) from Fulham in London. William was one of seven children born to Elizabeth and Henry. **Private Thomas Adams** (B.9), aged 20, was another 13/Royal Fusilier from nearby Hammersmith who came from a large family and was killed on 9 April 1917. You will also find men from the 12th Division who were killed on the same day as well as men from the Highland Light Infantry, Cameron Highlanders and Cameronians who fought with the 15th Division. The only officer here is **Lieutenant Charles Allen** (E.1) from the Canadian Field

Artillery who was killed in August 1918 along with **Driver Alexander Henry** (F.1) of the same unit.

Retrace your route to the main track and turn left to continue downhill to a crossroads. ❹ Directly ahead, in the distance – the ground to the left of the distinct water tower – is Orange Hill, from where the cavalry attack on Monchy-le-Preux was launched (see **Route 5**).

Turn left and in approximately 200m turn left again into Battery Valley along the Chemin des Fonds. There was no road here in 1917 but a German communication trench – **Hirson Lane** – followed the line of the

Nellie Adams pictured behind her brother's grave at Houdain Lane Cemetery after the war.

high bank – which will soon become evident to the right – up to the first right-hand bend. After the German offensive of March 1918 the British finally held on at this spot and their front line – **Feuchy Trench** – crossed the road from right to left – just before the bend – with **Feuchy Support** just behind.

The line of the bank became a track after the war but even by the early 1930s there was no through route to Feuchy.

Houdain Lane Cemetery.

As the road descends and begins to traverse the length of Battery Valley there are good views to be had of Houdain Lane Cemetery up the slope across to the left, whilst the slope to the right gets steeper. Whilst travelling through the valley consider for a moment the surprise felt by Captain Douglas Cuddeford as he advanced over the crest of Observation Ridge to see two batteries of German field guns of FAR 42 that he estimated were 200–300yd directly in front of him: 'For the second time that day – and we had to decide quickly this time – we found our safest direction lay right ahead; in fact our only course of action was to rush the guns, which we did ... and I think we got most of the Boche artillerymen'.

Imagine the scene: German gunners frantically attempting to reload after firing point blank into the advancing British troops and then, in what must have seemed like seconds for the German gunners at least, the Jocks of the 15th Division and the men of 5/Royal Berks from 35 Brigade were in and amongst them with the bayonet. Very few, we are told, managed to escape.

The remnants of German gun emplacements can still be seen today in the open ground and amongst the vegetation on the left-hand bend to the right of the road immediately before the right-hand bend that takes you back towards the railway arch at Spider Corner. **5** It is difficult to reconcile the tranquil scene which greets the visitor today with the scenes of violence that took place here on 9 April 1917.

Spider Corner is now ahead of you and after passing under the railway, your vehicle is a matter of metres away.

The former gun emplacements in Battery Valley can be seen on the left.

Route 3

Roeux

Coordinates: 50°18'11.32" N – 2°53'41.77" E
Distance: 3.0km/1.8 miles
Grade: Easy (total ascent 9.0m)
Suitable for: ♦ ♿ 🚗
Maps: Série Bleue 2406E – 99 Arras

General description and context: This is a route that combines a walk/ride with a short journey by vehicle before finally visiting two CWGC cemeteries, which is best done on foot. We have explained the sequence of attacks that took place on the Chemical Works at Roeux in some detail in **Route 8** and visitors are advised to familiarize themselves with what took place here before undertaking this short route.

In order to reduce what can be a confusing account of seven separate actions at Roeux, we have concentrated on the 101 Brigade attack of 28 April 1917.

Our route begins at the supermarket car park behind the railway station and visits the last vestiges of the former Château Lesage grounds and the memorial to 11/Suffolks, before locating the approximate area of the Mount Pleasant tunnel and caves. After visiting the site of the former communal cemetery and the church we return to the supermarket car park and drive along the access road to Crump Trench and Roeux cemeteries, which are reached after a short walk. Finally we visit Brown's Copse Cemetery.

Directions to start: Roeux is best approached from Arras on the D42. Drive through Fampoux and after crossing the TGV railway line and A1 Autoroute, turn right onto the D33 – Rue de la Gare – signposted, Monchy-le-Preux and Roeux *Centre*. Cross over the level crossing to find the supermarket car park on the left.

Route description: Park in the supermarket car park on the D33 ❶ which is a few metres south of the railway line and station buildings. If you stand in the car park looking towards the supermarket you

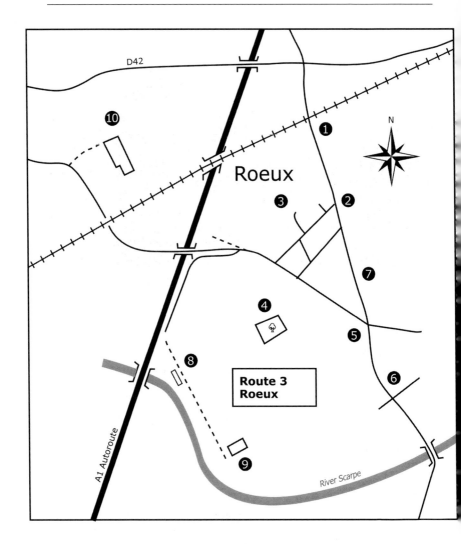

are on the site of the former Chemical Works – *Usine Chimique Lesage*. Nothing remains of the works today – except a patch of rough ground behind the supermarket – on what was a very large site which now includes the residential housing along Rue Résidence Robespierre further along the D33. This ground covers the remains of a military complex of bunkers and passageways that have been unused and unseen for over 100 years. The Chemical Works was the object of the disastrous 10 Brigade (4th Division) attack on 11 April 1917, an assault which was replicated the following day by two brigades

This supermarket has been built on the ground formerly occupied by the Chemical Works.

from the 9th (Scottish) Division attacking across the same ground with the same calamitous outcome; the *Official History* citing hurried preparation, inadequate reconnaissance and an ineffective artillery bombardment as reasons for the failure. The attack on 23 April 1917 was made by the 51st (Highland) Division, which grasped the Chemical Works only to be driven out again – despite the use of five tanks – by a dogged German counter-attack. What had clearly not been taken into account was that the village had been built over a system of caves which contributed to making its capture in 1917 an exceptionally difficult feat. The British attacks apparently took place without the knowledge that the system of caves and connecting tunnels allowed the defenders to reinforce their lines effectively, although it should be noted that several officers came very close to working out the cause of their repeated failures. Now dubbed by many as the 'Comical Works', on 23 April one 51st (Highland) Division diarist wrote that:

At every hour it seemed a voice from division announced a further attack on the Chemical Works by the highlanders. Each time they won it, and each time they were driven out ... There was no finish. Each time they went in they killed everything that was on the ground and each time, like dragon's teeth, the enemy sprang up again.

Leaving the site of the former chemical works, turn left down the main street – Rue Eugène Dumont – and walk down to Rue des Canadiens on the right. ❷ The road is marked by a small memorial to **Eugène Dumont**, a member of the resistance who was beheaded in November 1944 and who has given his name to the main street in Roeux. Turn right to find a large, ivy-covered German bunker which has been incorporated into a private garden. The bunker once sat in the open ground of the former Château Lesage and although the entrance is now bricked up, it gave access to the labyrinth of tunnels and caves beneath the village.

Rue des Canadiens is marked by the memorial to Eugène Dumont.

Continue along Rue des Canadiens and take the second turning on the right – **Rue Guy Lemaire**. Walk up the street until the bend to find a memorial ❸ to 11/Suffolks who attacked across this very ground on 28 April 1917. Launched at 4.25am, this attack involved Major General Cecil Nicholson's 34th Division with 103 Brigade

Now almost covered with ivy, the bunker which stood in the château grounds is one of the last remnants of the German occupation in 1917.

advancing north of the railway line and 101 Brigade to the south. The 11/Suffolks drew the château and Chemical Works, 10/Lincolns were in the centre and 15/Royal Scots the wooded area to the south of the village. The 16/Royal Scots – McCrae's Battalion, which won undying fame on 1 July 1916 near Contalmaison (see the authors' *A Visitor's Guide: The First Day of the Somme: Gommecourt to Maricourt*) – were detailed to follow the lead battalions and 'mop up' any remaining resistance. When the Suffolks moved forward they discovered thick, uncut barbed wire along the outer perimeter of the château. What followed was

The new memorial to 11/Suffolks.

carnage as the German machine-gunners picked off the Suffolk men as they struggled through the entanglements.

The idea of erecting a memorial gained momentum after a local resident came across the remains of a British soldier whilst digging the foundations for a new garden wall in a neighbouring property. The remains were subsequently reinterred at Terlincthun British Cemetery near Boulogne and classified as unknown. However, artefacts recovered from the burial site at Roeux indicated that they were those of **Lance Sergeant Charles Stevens** of A Company, 11/Suffolks, who was one of 103 men of his battalion killed in action that day. To this day the remains of some eighty-one Suffolks from that attack still lie beneath the ground between here and the former Chemical Works.

Retrace your route to Rue des Canadiens and turn right and after another 150m turn left into **Rue de Fampoux**. On your right, as you move down the road, is Mount Pleasant Wood on the crest of the rise ❹ which was bound in a tight triangle of trenches named **Cordite** – running from north–south between you and the wood – **Ceylon** to the north and **Colne** to the south after the British had finally taken Roeux. Ceylon Trench ran east – towards you – from Cordite, crossing Rue de Fampoux at the junction with **Rue Kaolac** before winding its way across Rue Eugène Dumont to the **Ceylon Cave complex**. The Mount Pleasant tunnel connected Cordite Trench with the **India Cave complex**, which was to the left of the road you are walking along and ran beneath the road in the vicinity of house number 18. The underground domain was used again during the Second World War by the villagers sheltering from shellfire and air raids. Today the Roeux caves are still accessible through the single entrance into the India Cave, but for reasons of safety remain closed to visitors. By December 1917 the caves were mostly occupied by the Guards Division whose subterranean occupation was marked by a profusion of graffiti, carvings and drawings.

Fortunately for the former **Private William Pethers**, who served with the Seaforth Highlanders, the Mount Pleasant Cave was still open to the curious when he revisited Roeux just before the outbreak of the Second World War in 1939. Writing in the *Lancashire Daily Post*, he recalled that the cave still ran from the old reserve line to the front line, east of the Chemical Works:

> Anyone who was at Roeux during '17 and '18 will remember Mount Pleasant Cave … I felt sure the cave would still be there but was not prepared to find what I actually did … I was told to see a M. Dumont who made me exceptionally welcome when I told him what I had come to see and, producing a bunch of keys, directed me to follow him. Round the side of his house was a complete dugout entrance, the door of which he unlocked. After lighting an acetylene lamp we entered and slithered down about 20 feet of chalky rubble and there I found myself back again in Mount Pleasant Cave.

A gifted musician and conductor, Pethers, who was at one time the personal conductor to Gracie Fields, was not present at Roeux during the 1917 fighting but was there as a 19-year-old when the German 1918 offensive swept through the village. He took over as conductor of the Coventry Hippodrome Orchestra in 1936 and died in Coventry in March 1978, aged 79.

Continue to the crossroads ❺ with the French war memorial on your left. The memorial records the award of the Croix de Guerre to the village in 1920 and contains an additional plaque dedicated to Eugène Dumont and his comrades. The triangular patch of ground behind the memorial was for many years the site of the communal cemetery, which was completely destroyed by shellfire. A new cemetery was later established 500m east on **Chemin de Croisette**.

On 28 April 1917, 10/Lincolns got as far as this spot and were followed by D Company of 16/Royal Scots. Both groups found

The ground behind the French memorial was previously the communal cemetery.

themselves enfiladed from both flanks with snipers active on their front. The German response was to mount a counter-attack, which was fortunately stopped near Mount Pleasant Wood.

Turn right and continue down the road past the *Mairie* to the Church of St Hilaire and stop near the crossroads. **6**

This is the furthest point reached by 16/Royal Scots of 101 Brigade although **Captain Gavin Pagan** and some of the 15th Battalion had even passed the church and dug in further east. A and B companies of 16/Royal Scots sustained heavy casualties as they entered the wooded area near the river some 200m or so south of here. **Captain Mike Lyon**, commanding A Company, proceeded to clear the buildings west of Rue du Pont – the road straight on, on the other side of the crossroads:

The Mairie *is situated a few metres from the church.*

The company was rather disorganized but they went looking for cellars etc. We took a few prisoners and I found myself with about a dozen men. We came across a lot of sniping from the top of the village, which B Company were mopping up … We got into the main street in driblets and had to take refuge from sniping behind some debris on each side of the road.

Second Lieutenant William Howat, a Rhodesian railway foreman in civilian life, could see 15/Royal Scots digging in about 200yd away. Conscious that he had to report to Major Alfred Warr and B Company at the church, he and his platoon ran into difficulties almost immediately:

We returned the fire and cleared the street, however, the Germans continued sniping at us. At this time Lieutenant [George] Henderson was shot in the hip and the Germans bombed us … We then tried to get along the river bank to the mill, from where we intended getting to the church. However, the firing was very heavy and it was only by running from shell hole to shell hole that we reached the mill.

He never made it. Howat and his men were eventually taken prisoner, as was Mike Lyon. Ordered to retire, the battalion could only muster eight officers and 201 other ranks at roll call that evening.

From the church, walk back up **Rue de la Mairie** – noting the plaque on the *Mairie* wall to seventeen residents of the commune of Roeux who were either shot, deported, died in captivity or otherwise killed during the Second World War – to the French memorial and bear right on to Rue Eugène Dumont. After approximately 200m stop. Beneath your feet, in the area of house number 18, ❼ is a tunnel which runs under the road and connects the **India Cave** complex to the extensive **Ceylon Cave** complex, still lying below ground to the right of the road.

Continue up the main street, passing Rue des Canadiens and the bunker on your left, to reach your vehicle in the supermarket car park.

From here it is a short drive to reach the two CWGC cemeteries situated on the far side of Mount Pleasant Wood. Turn left out of the car park, then second right along Rue des Canadiens. Turn right at the end and, after 150m, turn left onto a narrow minor road, following the CWGC signposts for Crump Trench ❽ and Roeux British ❾ cemeteries. The road bears sharp left before running parallel to the

A1 Autoroute. As you head south look across the fields to the left to see Mount Pleasant Wood.

The attack of 23 April 1917 formed up almost along the line of the present-day Autoroute, which practically obliterated the pre-war road layout. By 28 April the front line had advanced a mere 400m and encompassed Mount Pleasant Wood to run west of the château grounds before it crossed the railway line. Our road becomes a track for the final 300m and vehicles are best left by the metal gates where there is room to turn around. Proceed on foot towards the cemeteries.

Crump Trench British Cemetery
Crump Trench British Cemetery was made by fighting units between April and August 1917 and contains 215 Commonwealth burials, seventy-four of which are unidentified. There are also thirty-three special memorials. Eighty-five of the officers and men buried here died as a result of the fighting during April and May 1917 and of those, many are from the 51st (Highland) Division. **Second Lieutenant Thomas Wilson** (I.A.8) was only 26 years old when he was killed on 23 April whilst serving with 7/Argyll and Sutherland Highlanders. A former student at Fettes College in Edinburgh, he was commissioned in July 1915. Wounded early on in the attack on

Crump Trench British Cemetery.

Roeux, he insisted on remaining with his men. **Second Lieutenant Frederick Hislop** (II.B.13) was ten years older when he was killed on the same day whilst attached to the 7th Battalion. Gazetted in July 1916, he was a graduate of Glasgow University.

Hopes that the Germans might retire further to the east after the Chemical Works was finally taken on 3 May were dashed when, on the night of 15/16 May, after a heavy German bombardment, a fierce attack was launched along both sides of the railway line to the north of the village and on the village itself along the northern bank of the River Scarpe. These attacks initially met with some success until the Germans were eventually expelled, but not before they had inflicted heavy casualties on the defending units. **Lieutenant George Donaldson** (Sp. Mem. A.15), aged 31, was a former fish curer by trade and commissioned from the ranks in May 1915. Serving with 6/Gordon Highlanders, he was killed on 16 May 1917. Serving in the same battalion and also killed on 16 May was 24-year-old **Corporal Alexander Milne** (I.C.8), whose name appears on the family grave at Aberlour Cemetery in Scotland. Tragically, his sister Mary died on 21 June 1917 aged 21. Fourteen Seaforth Highlanders were victims of that attack, one of whom was 23-year-old **Private William Dunbar** (Sp. Mem. A.6), serving with A Company, 5/Seaforth Highlanders. A former shoe-maker by trade, his name appears on the Garmouth and Kingston Memorial in Scotland.

Finally, a name that many will recognize is that of Bonham-Carter and it is the great uncle of the actress Helena Bonham-Carter who lies in Plot II.C.7. **Second Lieutenant Norman Bonham-Carter** was aged 49 when he was killed on 3 May 1917, serving with the Household Battalion. One of his brothers, General Sir Charles Bonham-Carter, became Governor and Commander-in-Chief of Malta. Another brother, Sir Maurice Bonham-Carter, became private secretary to Herbert Asquith and married Asquith's daughter Helen. Sir Maurice was the grandfather of Helena Bonham-Carter.

Second Lieutenant Norman Bonham-Carter.

Roeux British Cemetery

Situated some 250m further along the track, Roeux British Cemetery was begun between April and November 1917. The cemetery contains 350 burials, thirty-one of which are unidentified, with a further eighty-two graves marked with special memorials. This is a battlefield cemetery closely associated with the 1917 attacks on Roeux. A casual glance at the dates on the majority of headstones will reveal 23 April, 28 April and 3 May 1917 and the men commemorated here of the 4th Division, the 34th Division and the 51st (Highland) Division give the cemetery a distinctly Scottish ambience. Sixty officers and men of 16/Royal Scots were killed on 28 April and of these, fifteen identified men are buried here. **CSM William Urquhart** (D.40), aged 30, was a veteran of the attack at la Boisselle on the Somme on 1 July 1916 where he was wounded. Returning to France in December 1916, he had been back in the line less than four months before he was killed on 28 April. **Private Robert 'Hamlet' MacMillan** (C.27), aged 41 and a dock labourer from Leith, was a serial defaulter during his previous service, a practice he continued during his enlistment in McCrae's Battalion. However, on the battlefield he was a different man and his death on 28 April was felt keenly amongst his comrades. His battalion is listed incorrectly by the CWGC as 15/Royal Scots.

Roeux British Cemetery.

Twenty identified men from 15/Royal Scots are buried here, many of whom were with **Captain Gavin Pagan** when he and his company were cut off beyond the church in Roeux. Pagan is commemorated on the Arras Memorial, but he is thought to be somewhere in the cemetery.

The eighty-one identified men of 10/Lincolnshire (Grimsby Chums) – many of whom had fought on the Somme – include 18-year-old **Lance Corporal Henry Haddon** (D.11) from Kettering, who was serving with B Company when he was killed on 28 April and 25-year-old **Second Lieutenant James Taylor** (C.10), who was commissioned in August 1915 and never lived to hear that his actions had earned him a Military Cross which was awarded posthumously on 1 July 1917. He is the only officer from the battalion buried here. Before you leave, find the headstone of 25-year-old **Private Anderson Jacklin** (D.48). He was a former farm labourer before he enlisted in 10/Lincolnshire at Grimsby in January 1915. He survived the disastrous action on 1 July at la Boisselle, where his battalion sustained 502 casualties out of 842 officers and men, his luck running out on 28 April 1917 during the attack on Roeux.

Leave the cemetery and return to your vehicle. If you wish to visit Brown's Copse Cemetery ❿ whilst you are in the vicinity, retrace your route to **Rue de Fampoux** and turn sharp left to drive over the A1 Autoroute, passing a minor road on your left, before taking the tunnels under the railway. The cemetery is to your right and accessed via a track. There is room to park and turn around.

Brown's Copse Cemetery
The original battlefield cemetery was greatly increased after the war by the addition of 850 burials (Plots V to VIII) brought in from the surrounding battlefields, bringing the total number of burials to 2,072 with just over a quarter remaining unidentified. The cemetery takes its name from the former Bois Rossignol which was situated almost where the large electricity pylon is today. Again there is a distinct Scottish character to the cemetery with a high proportion of burials from the 4th, 9th (Scottish) and 51st (Highland) divisions. In Plots I to IV you will find men killed during the fighting for Roeux and Greenland Hill, in particular there are 133 officers and men of 2/Seaforth Highlanders who were killed on 11 April 1917 during the attack on the Chemical Works. Probably the most well-known is 21-year-old **Lieutenant Donald Macintosh** (II.C.49), whose posthumous award of the Victoria Cross was gazetted in June 1917. A former student of Fettes College and Glasgow University, his

father was Assistant Director of Medical Services for the Lowland Divisional Area in Scotland. Five other 2/Seaforths officers are buried here, Second Lieutenants **William Dawson**, aged 28 (I.E.36), 33-year-old **Robert MacMillan** (II.E.7), 22-year-old **George Alexander** (I.D.42), 19-year-old **Phillip Grove** (III.D.28) and 20-year-old **Hugh Rose** (III.F.8).

The only officer from 1/Royal Irish Fusiliers, which attacked alongside the Seaforth Highlanders on 11 April 1917, is 19-year-old **Second Lieutenant Gerald Cullen** (III.D.6). He is one of forty Irish Fusiliers who died in the attack on Roeux. Killed with him was 23-year-old **Private Bernard McShane** (II.C.44), who was one of ten children from Holywood in Northern Ireland. Enlisting in Belfast, he had seen previous service with the Connaught Rangers and is also commemorated on the Holywood and District War Memorial.

The sixteen officers and men of 11/Suffolks who were killed in the attack on Roeux on 28 April, include **Lieutenant Dudley Miller** (I.A.33), who joined the battalion in August 1915 and 24-year-old **Second Lieutenant Hugh Grand** (I.D.29), a former banker's clerk who had been mentioned in despatches a month earlier. If you are looking for a headstone on which to place a cross of remembrance, then look no further than 20-year-old **Private Ernest Taylor** (I.C.13), who was employed in the horse-racing industry. Apart from his enlistment in Newmarket, little more is known of him, although his name does appear on the New Astley Club Memorial in Newmarket. Killed on 23 April was 23-year-old **Private William Hamilton** (II.B.18), of 7/Black Watch in 153 Brigade, who was one of almost 100 men from the battalion to die that day. Attacking on the left flank, the battalion was held up by heavy machine-gun fire near the Chemical Works, in what was described as one of 'the most fierce infantry battles the division had been involved in'. It is likely that Hamilton was one of the numerous casualties incurred at this time.

There are several RFC aircrew who were casualties of what became known as 'Bloody April' in the skies above Arras, when the German Air Service had the upper hand in terms of superiority of airworthy machines. **Captain Lionel Platt** (V.F.4), aged 31, and his observer, **Second Lieutenant Thomas Margerison** (V.F.1), were

Private William Hamilton.

flying a 57 Squadron FE2d and were shot down and killed over Vitry-en-Artois. Killed in a Spad VII from 19 Squadron on 29 April was the squadron commander, 26-year-old **Major Hubert Harvey-Kelly** (Sp. Mem. 7). Kelly achieved notoriety in 1914 when he was the first pilot to land in France, ahead of his squadron commander, Charles Burke. Life was short in those tempestuous days and Burke was killed on 9 April whilst in command of 1/East Lancashire Regiment. He is buried nearby in Point du Jour Military Cemetery. **Second Lieutenant Richard Kimbell** (Sp. Mem. 5), aged 19,

Major Hubert Harvey-Kelly.

was shot down over Roeux whilst flying a Nieuport 23; one of four 60 Squadron aircraft lost on 16 April.

Route 4
Telegraph Hill and 'The Harp'

Coordinates: 50°16'29.67" N – 2°48'59.71" E
Distance: 5.9km/3.6miles
Grade: Easy (total ascent 140m)
Suitable for: 🚲 🧍
Maps: Série Bleue 2406E – Arras

General description and context: The hinge of the old German line and the Hindenburg Line (*Siegfried Stellung*) was the village of Tilloy-lès-Mofflaines (Tilloy). South of the village lay **'The Harp'**, a formidable 'harp-shaped' position some 900m long by 450m at its widest point, with an additional fortification known as 'Noisy Redoubt' on the higher ground about 300m west of the modern day D37E. Along with **'Telegraph Work'**, to its immediate south The Harp's dominant position enabled German defenders to fire north towards Observation Ridge (see **Route 2**) and south towards Neuville-Vitasse, making it a vital piece in their defensive jigsaw. The capture of the village itself and the northern sector of The Harp were the responsibility of the 3rd Division (VI Corps), commanded by Major General Cyril Deverell. The southern portion of The Harp was allocated to the 14th (Light) Division (VII Corps), commanded by Major General Victor Couper, which, like the 3rd Division, had been allocated a number of tanks to assist with the attack. Both The Harp and Telegraph Hill – known as Mont de Tilloy on old French maps – were in British hands by 11.00am on 9 April 1917. Beginning in Tilloy this route takes us south, through the heart of The Harp and beyond, then turns east towards Shamrock Corner before using the D37E to return to Tilloy via the military cemetery.

Directions to start: Tilloy can be approached by using the D60 from Beaurains or the D393 from the centre of Arras. There is parking at Place Armand Duval near the crossroads in the village centre.

Route description: Tilloy was heavily defended by the Germans prior to the Battle of Arras but by the time the battalions of the

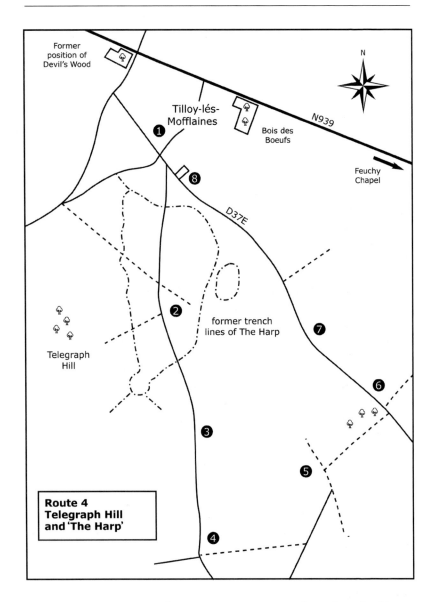

Former position of Devil's Wood

Tilloy-lés-Mofflaines

1

N939

Bois des Boeufs

Feuchy Chapel

8

D37E

2

former trench lines of The Harp

7

Telegraph Hill

6

3

5

Route 4
Telegraph Hill
and 'The Harp'

4

3rd Division went over the top on 9 April 1917, the village had been reduced almost to rubble by the artillery barrage that preceded the assault. The 3rd Division attack began with 1/Gordon Highlanders who reached their objective at 5.30am, followed by 10/Royal Welsh Fusiliers who secured the former **Devil's Wood** on the Black Line. The wood – the last vestiges of which can be seen south of the junction of the present day D939 and D60 – was the point at which the Hindenburg Line joined the original German front line. From his position east of the wood, **Private George Culpitt** watched the supporting battalions of 8 Brigade advance into Tilloy:

> We are now spectators of the battle which is taking place in front of us, and which we watch eagerly They reach the trench without difficulty and then go forward to the ruins of the village. Here they are lost to sight to reappear at intervals among the piles of bricks and stone which were once houses.

Apart from one or two pockets of resistance which were overcome by 9 Brigade, the surviving garrison from RIR 76 felt that surrender was infinitely preferable to the alternative and as the 3rd Division's attack moved inexorably towards Feuchy Chapel the village was left in British hands. Of the six tanks of 9 Company, C Battalion, that had been assigned to support the attack, one did assist in the final capture of the village. **Gunner William Dawson** was in Tank C/50: 'We did manage to get along engaging the enemy and had the satisfaction of taking part in the capture of Tilloy … Unfortunately we ran into a very bad patch on the outskirts of Tilloy and became stuck with the tank resting on its belly and the tracks going round uselessly.'

From your vehicle ❶ head southeast along the D37 – signposted Wancourt. Bear right at the fork in the road and head towards Neuville-Vitasse and the *Centre Sportif*. You are now heading along Rue de Neuville and in 300m will pass the sports centre buildings on the left. Stop by the football pitch, which has been built on the northerly aspect of The Harp trench system. To your right the line swung northwest and to the left it cut straight across the football pitch towards the D37E. Running some 20m or so to the right of the road was a trench line called – obviously perhaps – The String which ran down the centre of The Harp from north to south and our route follows this line for the next 600m. To enable you to appreciate the extent of The Harp we have marked its outline on the route map.

After the last house on the right the road narrows and heads towards a line of pylons. You are still within the 3rd Division sector and it was from right to left across this ground that the attacking battalions of 9 Brigade advanced. On the extreme right flank were 4/Royal Fusiliers:

> W Company, leading on the right, suffered very heavily from rifle and machine gun fire, and also partly from our own

barrage. All the officers were wounded, Captain [Bernard Finnie] severely, and command devolved on Second Lieutenant the Earl of Shannon who, though wounded, led the company from Nomeny Trench [200m out in the fields to the right] and was the first man to enter String Trench. Z Company were caught by fire from the north-east corner of Tilloy village, but, with the help of two platoons of X, assisted in the capture of [Linx] and String Trenches. Captain [Alvan Ewen] Millson (CO, X Company) was mortally wounded as he entered the latter ... X and Y companies supported the two assaulting companies mopped up Nomeny Trench and carried the battalion forward to the final objective.

The Royal Fusiliers' war diarist stated that 'One tank came up and sat on NOMENY TR. after the Battn had passed through but except for the moral support the tanks were of no assistance owing to the state of the ground.'

A 'minimum' of five German officers and seventy other ranks were captured along with three machine guns, two *minenwerfer* and four *granatenwerfer* but the battalion had suffered heavily: Second Lieutenant William Paddock, like Captain Millson, died of wounds and a further seven officers were wounded. CWGC records indicate that forty-seven other ranks died on 9 April 1917; 126 were wounded.

Sadly, 19-year-old Richard Bernard Boyle, the 7th Earl of Shannon, who had led W Company to its objectives on 9 April, was killed four days later. His body was never recovered and he is remembered on Bay 3 of the Arras Memorial to the Missing and the war memorial designed by Sir Edwin Lutyens in the churchyard of St John the Baptist Church, Busbridge in Surrey.

At the crossroads continue straight ahead, keeping the wooded crown of Telegraph Hill on your right. Just before you reach the track on the right, ❷ leading towards Telegraph Hill, you will cross the divisional boundary between the 3rd and 14th divisions. The initial assault of the 14th Division was made against the southern sector of The Harp and the formidable defences of Telegraph Hill. Major General Victor Couper had deployed 42 Brigade on the left and 43 Brigade on the right with support from tanks of 8 Company, C Battalion. Two tanks did manage to reach the German front line – **Second Lieutenant Thomas Toshack** in C/29 (No. 597) and **Second Lieutenant R.C. Wareham** in C/23 (No. 582) both covered the advance of the infantry and fired on German infantry in Pol Trench until Wareham's 'bus' was bombed and threw a track and in going to assist Toshack's tank became ditched and was heavily shelled. We will meet Lieutenant Toshack again in **Route 5**. **Second Lieutenant Philip Saillard's** tank – C/24 (No. 777), named *Charlie Chaplin* – reached the Blue Line before becoming 'bellied' on the western edge of Noisy Work. In all, six of 8 Company, C Battalion's tanks became 'ditched' – three of them in String Trench – and the others suffered some form of battle damage. **Second Lieutenant James Cameron's** C/39 (No. 599) taking a direct hit. Cameron – who had already earned the MC – survived and went on to earn a bar to his MC and the DSO during 1918. He died in 1955.

Walking across The Harp after the battle had been concluded it became obvious to Major John 'Boney' Fuller, a staff officer with 1 Tank Brigade, that for some tank crews it had been a very short baptism of fire: 'I found one tank standing out of a trench with its tail end resting on the bottom of it. On looking through the sponson door, I saw the driver sitting upright in his seat. He was beheaded.'

Turn right and walk up the track towards Telegraph Hill and after a short distance the D60 becomes visible on the right with the buildings of Arras beyond. After 170m you will see another track on the right, this is the point where the western edge of The Harp ran east of Telegraph Hill towards Telegraph Work. If you stop here you can see the whole of Telegraph Ridge stretching away towards the east.

The wooded area on the summit of Telegraph Hill.

The road south of The Harp with Neuville-Vitasse church spire in the distance. The Hindenburg Line ran to the left of the road.

Retrace your route to the junction and turn right to continue walking slightly downhill along the 'String' of The Harp. The point at which the road begins to level off and passes directly beneath power lines is the approximate position of the main Hindenburg Line which continued across the fields to your left to run to the east of Neuville-Vitasse and beyond. Stop here ❸ and look across towards Telegraph Hill. You will notice a rough farm track to the right at this point which makes a right-hand dog leg into the field. Looking along that track and slightly to the right towards a stand of trees you should be able to make out a pill-box on the slope of the hill in the area of what was the **Preussen Work** or **Redoubt**, roughly marking the German front-line system of 9 April 1917. It is marked 'Abri' on modern IGN maps. You are now looking over the ground across which **Captain Oswold Benbow-Rowe** and men of B Company, 5/King's Shropshire Light Infantry (KSLI) advanced south of The Harp. His orders were to capture a section of the Hindenburg Line between two communication trenches named **'Eye Lane'** and **'Dog Lane'** in the fields to your left:

> Slight resistance was encountered in Telegraph Hill Trench and Head Lane but this was immediately overcome and my

company captured between 50–70 prisoners here … Germans in dugouts were cleared out by 9.10am and work was started in consolidating the line. I captured and consolidated this line with the remnants of A, B and C Companies. D Company had meantime obtained their objective in Silent Work [just southeast of Noisy Work] and by 10.00am communication had been established with the Suffolks on their left and the Ox and Bucks Light Infantry in the String and Negrine Trench.

Now look across into the fields to the left of the road. This is where the remnants of A, B and C companies strengthened the line, a mere 400m away from where you are standing. But it wasn't as straightforward as Benbow-Rowe suggests; records indicate that twelve officers and 189 other ranks from 5/KSLI were killed or wounded during the assault, just under a third of its strength.

Continue along the track until you reach a crossroads with a small copse on the right. Turn left here (the road is marked *privé* but the authors have had no difficulty and many local dog owners regularly use the track). ❹ For the first 300m or so the track runs along the approximate line of the divisional boundary with the 56th (London) Division which was tasked with capturing Neuville-Vitasse. After 250m you will cross the Hindenburg Line at **Telegraph Hill Trench** which runs down from where Captain Benbow-Rowe broke into the German line to the east of Neuville-Vitasse.

The track continues straight ahead to a crosstracks where a left turn will take you up a gentle hill and round a left-hand bend. About halfway up the hill a track on the right ❺ follows the course of the former **Airy Trench** and takes you towards a small copse. Note that after some 250m you will cross what became the German front line – which included sections of Airy Trench and **Airy Work**, a little further up the slope to your left – after the German Mars offensive, launched on 28 March 1918, had finally ground to a halt three days later.

At the northeastern end of the copse you will meet the D37E road at **Shamrock Corner**. ❻ This point was effectively the limit of the advance on 9 April 1917 in this sector. You are now back in the area held by the 3rd Division at that time and if you stand at the junction, with the copse on your left and face the road, **Shamrock Trench** was almost immediately in front of you with **Shamrock Road** a few metres to its right. Both of these features are long gone but as you now turn left and head up the road towards Tilloy, a track which was called **Chapel Road** will appear after 30m on the right. This track

'Shamrock Corner' where the track meets the D37E. A track ran southeast across the fields on the opposite side but no longer exists. The track to Feuchy Chapel runs east across the fields in the distance, centre left, as indicated by the distinct line between the crops.

leads to **Airy Corner** – the junction of the track with the D37 – and then Feuchy Corner before reaching **Feuchy Chapel** on the D939. The 4/Royal Fusiliers were in position in shell holes at Airy Corner on 3 May where they received orders to advance to positions just south of the Arras–Cambrai Road. It takes little imagination to see – in the mind's eye – the long line of men marching along the track in company formation led by **Lieutenant Colonel Edward North** and his adjutant, **Second Lieutenant Keith Markby**.

Continue up the gentle rise of the D37E and stop where the line of electricity cables crosses the road. If you face the road in the direction of Tilloy, Telegraph Hill is on your left and on either side of the road are the remains of two German concrete pill-boxes. ❼ At first sight what appear to be machine-gun apertures facing east are probably *blinkstelle* for light signalling to observation posts at command centres at Feuchy Chapel and other sections of the Wancourt–Feuchy Line on the slightly higher ground to the east. These pill-boxes were captured by 14/Londons (London Scottish) on 9 April 1917.

All was reversed here on 28 March 1918 during the German Mars offensive when the German tide drove the British line south

One of two German concrete pill-boxes on either side of the Wancourt road – the D37E. This example – with large blinkstelle *(signalling) aperture clearly visible – is to the west of the road looking northwest. The wood on the summit of Telegraph Hill can be seen directly above.*

of the River Scarpe back some 2 miles, recapturing part of the old Hindenburg Line and the village of Neuville-Vitasse. The German attack crossed the road from right to left here and was finally held about 100m into the fields to your left, on the line of what was **Bill Trench**. The new front line then ran southwest from here to loop around the northern fringes of Neuville-Vitasse, the church spire of which you can see in the distance over your left shoulder.

Just 150m further on the German front line of April 1918 – **Ayr Trench** – crossed the road here then curved northeast becoming **Orkney Trench** to run in front of the **Bois des Boeufs**, up ahead to your right. From there the German front line ran across the fields towards the pylons astride the line of the D939 Route de Cambrai.

A little further along you will see a farm track on the right. This is the **Chemin de la Chapelle** which leads to a junction with the D939, west of Feuchy Chapel. In the late spring and early summer of 1918 a German salient centred on **Orkney** and **Aberdeen trenches** – and studded with sentry posts, machine guns and bomb blocks – straddled the track some 220m from this point. It was from this area on 11 April 1918 that the Germans attacked and drove in a post of 8/Middlesex in **Tilloy Trench**, some 300m into the fields on your left, causing it to withdraw, although the post was recovered by 4.30pm the same day. On the following day **Second Lieutenant Harley Lionel Adrian Oswald-Hicks** of the same battalion, a keen footballer and all-round athlete who had been educated at Tottenham Grammar School, was shot and it was a pre-war professional footballer, **Private Edward 'Fred' Didymus**, who attempted a rescue mission on the day before his 33rd birthday.

Born in Southsea, Portsmouth on 13 April 1885, Fred Didymus played as a forward for 'Pompey', his home-town club, before moving to Northampton Town in 1907 where he scored two goals in nine appearances. In 1908 he joined Huddersfield Town, scoring five goals in thirty appearances, before moving again in 1909 to play a handful of games for Blackpool and finally ending his career with Port Vale the following year. He returned to Portsmouth in 1911 and worked as a tram driver before leaving wife Mary and children George, Hilda, Harold and Irene to join the army in December 1915. Not posted to France until 1918, he arrived on 24 March and joined 8/Middlesex two days later. When Second Lieutenant Oswald Hicks was hit on 12 April the ex-professional footballer did not hesitate. The battalion chaplain wrote to Didymus' wife, who was six months pregnant:

> His death was so gallant that to me it was one of inspiration and thankfulnesss. His officer was sniped in front of his post, and your husband immediately went forward to try to recover him. He met with a similar misfortune. We got the body down in the evening, and I buried him in a military cemetery.

Didymus' fifth child, Norman, was born in July 1918, three months after his father had been killed but sadly died, aged just twelve weeks.

Continue for another 500m or so. It was here that **Tilloy Trench** – the British front line in April 1918 – crossed the road and ran off to the northeast. Some 250m off into the fields on your left was the site of Noisy Work where Second Lieutenant Sailliard's tank, *Charlie Chaplin*, bellied at the western edge and was then hit by a trench mortar and set on fire. Philip Saillard – an old boy of Haileybury School – survived the Harp fighting but died of wounds – aged 19 – on 22 August 1917 during the Third Battle of Ypres.

Across to your right is the wooded expanse of the Bois des Boeufs where 13/King's Liverpool Regiment was held up on 9 April 1917 after the failure of the expected tank support. Eventually the position was taken, enabling 8 Brigade to advance towards the Wancourt–Feuchy Line. From here 2/Royal Scots and 7/Somerset Light Infantry (SLI) advanced parallel with the D939 coming under fire from the heavily fortified area around Feuchy Chapel. The Royal Scots historian documented the point at which the advance was halted:

> By the time Chapel road was reached, this fire was so intense that the left of the Brigade could make no progress. The Royal Scots, veering to the south, managed to push forward some distance and seized another hostile trench, but at this point they were subjected to terrific machine-gun fire from the south as well as the north. It was suicide to continue the advance.

On 28 March 1918, during the German Operation Mars offensive, 6/Cameron Highlanders were in support east of Feuchy Chapel in **Halifax** and **Dagger** trenches and 13/Royal Scots were forced back by the German advance. Gradually the 45 Brigade units withdrew along the line of the D939 to take up new positions around Telegraph Ridge. As the Cameron Highlanders fell back they reported that 'throughout all this period the enemy was suffering enormous casualties from our rifle and Lewis gun fire, the men thoroughly realizing the value of their rifles and the value of the Lewis gun was more than ever demonstrated'. Withdrawing to the Army Line trenches, which ran west of the Bois des Boeufs, **Second Lieutenant Archibald Macmillan**, a recently commissioned pre-war regular, led a counter-attack into the wood, expelling about twenty German infantrymen and establishing an outpost line just to the east; adding an MC to his MM. This was the closest point to Arras reached by the Mars offensive. Looking straight ahead you can see the outskirts of Tilloy and to the right of the road is the red-tiled roof of the shelter at Tilloy British Cemetery ❽ with a large *calvaire* – which used to be surrounded by pollarded limes and a low yew hedge – standing outside the cemetery walls.

Tilloy British Cemetery
The wooded area which borders the northeastern edge of the cemetery should not be confused with the Bois des Boeufs, which stands 600m to the northeast. The cemetery was begun in April 1917 and Rows A to H in Plot I are largely battlefield burials. The remaining graves in Plot I, and others in the first three rows of Plot II, represent later fighting in 1917 and the first three months of 1918 and

The calvaire *standing outside Tilloy British Cemetery. The Cross of Sacrifice in the cemetery can be seen on the left.*

the clearing of the village in August 1918. These 390 original burials were increased after the Armistice when graves were brought in from the surrounding battlefields. One of these may have been 30-year-old **Second Lieutenant Andrew Birrel** (VI.B.21) who was killed on 9 April serving with 6/KOSB and went 'over the top' with 27 Brigade near the Cuthbert and Clarence mine craters northeast of St-Laurent-Blangy, which we feature in **Route 1** in our companion guide book *The Battles of Arras – North*. Today there are 1,642 casualties buried here, of which 611 are unidentified. Amongst the special memorials is one that commemorates eleven men of 6/KOSB whose graves were destroyed by shellfire.

Resting in the first row as you enter the cemetery is ex-professional footballer **Fred Didymus**, who was killed on 12 April 1918 just a few hundred metres from this spot trying to recover the body of his officer, **Second Lieutenant Harley Oswald-Hicks**, who had been sniped a little earlier. Didymus (I.AA.12) and the man he tried to save (II.H.7) now lie in the same cemetery in perpetuity, a short 60m walk apart.

The battlefield burials reflect the actions of the 3rd and 14th divisions on 9 April 1917. There are forty-nine identified men from the two 8 Brigade battalions, **7/KSLI** and **2/Royal Scots** and thirty-seven from **4/Royal Fusiliers** (9 Brigade).

One of those Royal Fusiliers is **Lance Corporal Sutton Jubilee Sparkes** (IV.F.22), of Guist in Norfolk whose birth year – coinciding as it did with Queen Victoria's Golden Jubilee in 1887 – prompted his mother and father, Alfred and Emily Sparkes, to bestow upon him an interesting middle name.

Amongst the twenty-two men of the **East Yorkshire Regiment** are three subalterns, the youngest of whom, 19-year-old **Second Lieutenant John Tyrrell** (II.H.28), was killed by a sniper near The Harp. **Second Lieutenants Frederick Prince** (I.A.26) and **William Hoyle** (I.B.23), both aged 20, were both killed by machine-gun fire directed from the Feuchy Chapel area. The 5/Oxford and Bucks Light Infantry was a 42 Brigade battalion attacking south of The Harp and all but five of the fifty men of the battalion buried here were killed on 9 April. Amongst these was 18-year-old **Private Frederick Hall** (III.E.4) from Reading, who was one of six children born to Rosa and Ernest Hall. His elder brother, Private Ernest Hall, was killed on 14 March 1917 serving with 2/Royal Berkshires. The vast majority of the thirty-seven identified Canadians buried here were killed between 26 and 28 August 1918, during the final Allied advance. One of them, 21-year-old **Private Albert Fenwick DCM** (II.B.5) of Enterprise, Ontario, was killed whilst serving with 21/Battalion on 26 August during heavy fighting for the Drocourt–Quéant Line. During the Battle of Amiens eighteen days earlier, Fenwick and **Private Archie McPhee** – born in Michigan, USA – had continued to fight forward with their Lewis gun despite losing the rest of their crew and succeeded in capturing no less than seven German machine guns, an officer and twelve men near Marcelcave; Fenwick and McPhee later being seen 'with their helmets askew loaded with souvenirs and fortified with Hun refreshments simply eating up the town, the very personification of the Canadian conquering spirit'. Both men were awarded the DCM on 18 November 1918 for their actions on 8 August. On the same day Fenwick was killed McPhee – probably still working a Lewis with Fenwick – was severely wounded; his left foot being blown off and right leg severed at the knee. Both legs were amputated the same day but McPhee survived to return home to Canada in 1919 and lived for another forty-one years.

Interestingly there are several men buried here who fell on the opening day of the Battle of the Somme on 1 July 1916 and who seem, geographically at least, out of place. These include one Accrington

Pal of 11/East Lancashire – 19-year-old **Private Arthur Dent** of Burnley (VII.B.10) – and two Barnsley Pals – 31-year-old ex-miner **Private Walter Swift**, 13/York and Lancs (1st Barnsley) (VII.A.4) and **Private William Hague** of Dodworth, an early recruit to 14/York and Lancs (2nd Barnsley) (VIII.B.15) – all of whom fell in the 31st Division's disastrous assault on the village fortress of Serre, 23km (14 miles) to the southwest as the shell flies. Quite why the remains of these men were transported to and buried in Tilloy is puzzling as the bodies of all three pals were recovered in 1921 from the heart of the Serre battlefield of 1 July 1916, all of them identified from information on spoons found with their bodies. Dent's remains were recovered from a spot near what had been the German front line opposite Matthew Copse, Hague's were found between the German first and second line trenches opposite Luke Copse, whilst Swift's body – identified by the following titles on a spoon '890 1.B.Y&L' – was found with several others by the track which now leads up to Sheffield Memorial Park: a location which had been the British second trench. The story of the attack on Serre is told in the authors' *A Visitor's Guide: The First Day of the Somme: Gommecourt to Maricourt*.

Rather eerily for one of the authors, another man buried here shares the same initials and surname. Second Lieutenant J.A. Cooksey (I.D.22) was killed on 1 May 1917 along with another officer and four men of 116/Siege Battery RGA. All six men now lie in a row. Born in West Bromwich in 1887, Joseph Arnold Cooksey's mining engineer father emigrated to Natal in South Africa with his family before the war, Joseph going on to become an engineer on the South African railways. Cooksey is recorded on the South African Roll of Honour and his name also appears on the University of Birmingham's war memorial in its Aston Webb building. Cooksey's brother, Wilfred Maurice Cooksey of B Special Company, Royal Engineers, was killed less than three weeks earlier and is buried in Barlin Communal Cemetery Extension, south of Béthune.

Leave the cemetery and continue along Rue de Wancourt to the crossroads and your vehicle.

Route 5

Monchy-le-Preux

Coordinates: 50°16′15.35″ N – 2°53′37.28″ E
Distance: 4.5km/2.8 miles
Grade: Easy (total ascent 50m)
Suitable for: 🚶 🚴
Maps: Série Bleue 2506O – Rouvroy/Vitry-en-Artois

General description and context: Although we concentrate on the events of 11 April 1917 during this route, we do look briefly at the fight around Infantry Hill on 14 April and have provided a brief overview of events in **Route 8**. The hill-top village of Monchy-le-Preux (Monchy) was, in many ways, the key to the 1917 Arras offensive; indeed the strategic plan for the first day's fighting included the capture of this village which dominated the Arras battlefield. By the close of the first day on 9 April, however, the British attack had ground to a halt, still to the west of the village, and a resumption of the attack was scheduled for 11 April. Our route retraces that taken by the cavalry on entering the village before examining Infantry Hill and the Mound and the events leading up to **Lieutenant Colonel James Forbes-Robertson**'s defence of the village.

The 37th Division – with support from the 15th and 3rd divisions to left and right – were tasked with taking Monchy during a period of heavy snow on 11 April. The 111 Brigade would advance on the village with 3 Cavalry Division in support, together with six tanks from 8 Company, C Battalion, 1 Tank Brigade, of which only four made it past the start line to engage the Germans. The 5.00am attack was handicapped by disorganized artillery support due to a late handover between artillery units, prompting XV Artillery Brigade to ask for a postponement of zero hour. This request appears not to have reached the supporting units, leaving a frustrated **Brigadier General Charles Compton**, commanding 111 Brigade, to proceed without knowing who was supporting his infantry: 'At 5.00am when the attack started my brigade had no artillery support, and I did not know what batteries had been allotted to me, or who was commanding them.'

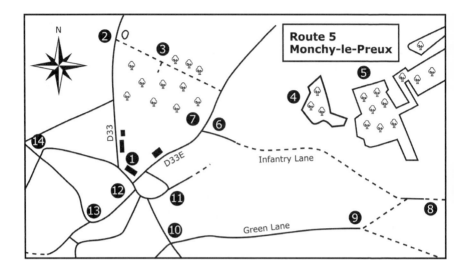

In the opinion of the officer commanding the C Battalion tanks, at least two of them were hit in what was believed to be a confusion of friendly and enemy fire, one of which was Tank C/36 (No. 600) commanded by **Second Lieutenant Charles Fredrick Nelson Ambrose**. With his tank badly damaged to the south of the village near the road to Wancourt and with all his gunners wounded, Ambrose continued to keep up a fire on German soldiers intent on surrounding his machine and attacking it with grenades, a feat for which he was awarded the DSO on 18 June 1917.

Lieutenant George Salter's C/21 (No. 578) – named *The Perfect Lady* – and **Second Lieutenant Thomas Toshack's** C/29 (No. 597) entered Monchy where they joined **Second Lieutenant Henry Watt Johnston's** C/26 (No. 787) and proceeded along the main street, forcing the Germans to seek cover and pull back. At 6.30am a British barrage fell on the village and disabled *The Perfect Lady* killing the signaller and wounding four other crewmen. C/26 broke down and was also caught in the barrage and abandoned. A sad fate befell C/29, which escaped destruction in the village, but was set on fire near the woods to the northwest. Only three crewmen escaped and **Second Lieutenant Thomas Toshack** is commemorated on the Arras Memorial along with eight other men of C Battalion, Heavy Branch Machine Gun Corps who died on 11 April. If the question is asked 'who took Monchy on 11 April?', then the answer has to be 'the tanks of C Battalion' in that they suppressed the German defenders and allowed the British infantry to advance.

By 8.00am 13/King's Royal Rifle Corps and 13/Rifle Brigade, with two battalions of Royal Fusiliers in support, moved quickly through the village, linking up with the 15th (Scottish) Division, which had lost direction and had veered into Monchy from the north. **Sergeant Rupert Whiteman**, serving with 10/Royal Fusiliers, recalled that there appeared to be representatives from almost every regiment in the British Army in the village: 'Along the street and up the hill the crowd surged. It was a similar crowd that one sees issuing from the gates after a football match. All bayonets had been fixed before getting out of the trench but I don't think anyone had the occasion to use them.'

With Monchy captured, the leading squadrons of 8 Cavalry Brigade, who had been waiting on Orange Hill, entered the village from the northwest with the intention of clearing the ground to the north. The Essex Yeomanry arrived in the village square along **Rue de la Gaieté** and then headed out on the D33 north towards Pelves, whilst 10/Royal Hussars entered the square via **Hussar Lane**, turning northeast along the D33E. Both regiments met heavy machine-gun fire, **Lieutenant Colonel Phillip Hardwick**, commanding 10/Royal Hussars, was wounded and the cavalry got no further than the château grounds before the German counter-barrage turned Monchy into an inferno.

What is often absent from accounts of the fight for Monchy is the part played by the 37th Divisional Cavalry: the Northamptonshire Yeomanry. They had also been on Orange Hill that morning and, according to their war diary, as soon as 8 Cavalry Brigade had passed through them they received orders to advance on Monchy and clear the woods to the northeast. **Sergeant Cyril Day**, riding with B Squadron, had vivid memories of that gallop from Orange Hill: 'We went on a gallop, the enemy simply pouring shells at us. It was a wonderful sight, the ground was covered with snow, the air keen and frosty and the sun shining making the breath of hundreds of horses look like smoke pouring from machine guns.'

Entering the village from the northwest, they came face-to-face with the carnage that had been unleashed by the German barrage. The streets of Monchy were littered with dead men and horses and the gutters ran red with blood: it was an appalling sight. Alan Thomas, a company commander serving with 6/Royal West Kents, described the scene he found on 12 April:

The sight that greeted me was so horrible I almost lost my head. Heaped on top of one another and blocking up the roadway for as far as one could see, lay the mutilated bodies of our men and their horses. These bodies, torn and gaping, had stiffened into fantastic attitudes. All the hollows of the road were filled with blood. This was the cavalry.

In the circumstances there was little the Northamptonshire men could do amidst the slaughter and, in order to prevent needless casualties, they were ordered to retire. It was during this retirement that a cousin of one of the authors, **Captain Gerald 'Gerry' Murland**, was awarded the MC for tending wounded men under shellfire and leading them back through the barrage to the shelter of Happy Valley. Despite their brief entry into Monchy, the regiment reported fourteen men killed and sixty-one wounded with over 170 horses being killed or wounded.

Meanwhile, **Lieutenant Colonel Francis Whitmore**, Essex Yeomanry, took command and set about organizing the defence of Monchy. Although the Germans massed for a counter-attack on several occasions they were repeatedly driven off, **Lance Corporal Harold Mugford**, Essex Yeomanry, was partly responsible for this, and despite his injuries, continued to fire his Hotchkiss gun until he was taken to a dressing station, where he was wounded yet again. His award of the Victoria Cross was gazetted in November 1917. By the time the cavalry had been relieved by the Royal West Kents on the evening of 12 April, there was very little of the village left standing and they were without **Brigadier General Charles Bulkeley Johnson**, commanding 8 Cavalry Brigade, who had been killed on 11 April.

Directions to start: Monchy-le-Preux is east of Arras, just north of the D939. From the north it can be reached from Roeux on the D33. Park in the village square opposite the *Mairie*.

Route description: The village square is dominated by the former château building, ❶ which is now a school, but in April 1917 it was used by **Captain William Wood**, the 10/Royal Hussars' medical officer, as an aid station. It was here that **Lieutenant Bill Murland**, the brother of Gerry Murland and another cousin of one of the authors, was brought after he had been wounded in the leg in the château grounds. Seven officers of the Hussars were wounded with a further two dying of their wounds, together with twenty-four other ranks killed and 130 wounded.

The château building at Monchy where Captain William Wood established his aid centre.

With the château building immediately in front of you turn left onto the D33, signposted Roeux and Gavrelle. As the road bends round to the right and heads downhill, look across to the road on your left – **Rue de la Gaieté**. This is the road along which the advanced squadron of the Essex Yeomanry entered the village before turning down the D33 towards Roeux – the direction you are now heading. As you continue downhill there are excellent views over the Scarpe Valley to be had: Fampoux can be seen on the left and Roeux to the right. **Captain Douglas Cuddeford** of 12/Highland Light Infantry had looked left – over towards Orange Hill – and saw the cavalry advance that morning: 'Away behind us, moving quickly in extended order down the slope of Orange Hill, was line upon line of mounted men covering the whole extent of the hillside as far as we could see. It was a thrilling moment for us infantrymen.'

Just imagine for a moment now the horsemen of the Essex Yeomanry clattering down this very road heading towards Pelves to capture Pelves Mill and secure the ridge northeast of Monchy. The château grounds were not so thickly wooded in 1917, so the German machine-gunners would have seen the yeomen galloping along the road.

The turning off the D33 leading along the northern edge of the château park.

At the bottom of the hill a pond ❷ marks the position of a track on the right, which leads along the northern edge of the wood. It was at this point that the Essex Yeomanry veered sharply to the right and along this track in an attempt to avoid the hail of machine-gun bullets. There must have been casualties here and one can imagine the shouts and screams and the whinnying of horses and the wounded attempting to crawl into the shelter of the trees.

Turn right along the track – just as the Essex Yeomanry did – to pass a concrete bench on the right. Ignore the tracks leading into the wood and, at the point where the trees cover both sides of the track, stop. ❸ It was here that the Essex Yeomanry turned right into the wood to take up positions in the château grounds, where they met the advanced squadron from 10/Royal Hussars. Two strongpoints were established, one in the château grounds and the other at the northeastern exit to the village.

Continue along the track to reach the junction with the D33E – Rue de Pelves. Across the fields straight ahead of you is Arrow Head Copse, ❹ behind which are the Twin Copses ❺ where the Germans were seen to be massing on several occasions, although no serious counter-attack ever materialized from this direction. This was the high ground which 8 Cavalry Brigade had been ordered to capture.

Lance Corporal Mugford was in the fields to the left of the turning to Infantry Lane on the D33E.

The château park to your right is now almost totally obscured by trees, but in 1917 you would have seen men of 10/Royal Hussars manning two machine guns and firing towards Arrow Head and Twin Copses. This is where Lieutenant Bill Murland ❼ was positioned and where he was wounded. He was not alone. Captain Douglas Cuddeford recalled what he witnessed within that very woodland that day:

> An extensive orchard belonging to the big chateau farm on the north side of the village was full of dead and wounded men of our 45th Brigade ... While the snow was falling . . some of us went out to give what help we could to the many ... lying about in the open ... As we moved through the orchard ... too many of them lay still like hummocks of snow... . one of these hummocks heaved and cracked open ... as a poor kilted Highlander turned over at the sound of our voices ... His bare thigh was only a blackened stump.

It was somewhere near this spot too that Douglas Cuddeford witnessed the death of 49-year-old Brigadier Charles Bulkeley-Johnson, the commander of 8 Cavalry Brigade, sometime between 9.00am and midday:

The Brigadier thought he would like to see something of the enemy dispositions for himself, and I told him it could be done, but that to reach a point of vantage on the low ridge in front … the greatest caution was required, and that if the German snipers spotted us it would be necessary to dodge them by sprinting diagonally from shell hole to shell hole … Nevertheless the General insisted on going against my advice … and he would insist on walking straight on. I led the little procession, and … as soon as we reached the ridge, a fusillade of bullets hummed around our ears. We had not gone far when one skimmed past me and struck the General full on the cheek bone. I shall never forget his piercing shriek as he tumbled down and rolled over on the ground.

Cuddeford later went out to recover Bulkeley-Johnson's body and took it back to the support line where he sat, idly contemplating it whilst 'watching the snowflakes settling gently on the blue upturned dead face, with its grizzled moustache'. Bulkeley-Johnson's ADC, **Captain Eric Hardy**, who also went on the reconnaissance, wrote in a letter that the general had been 'shot through the heart and lungs'. Charles Bulkeley-Johnson lies today in Gouy-en-Artois Communal Cemetery Extension, 15km southwest of Arras (Grave A.30).

Turn right at the junction and follow the road uphill to where the road curves round to the right with a track on the left. Stop here and look across to your left into the fields. This is the approximate spot ❻ where **Lance Corporal Harold Mugford** of 8 Squadron, Machine Gun Corps (Cavalry) kept up a withering fire on Arrow Head and the Twin Copses with his Hotchkiss gun. After the Essex Yeomanry had occupied Monchy, Mugford had galloped forward and set up his Hotchkiss gun in this exposed position to fire on Germans massing for a counter-attack. 'It was quite the most glorious sensation I have ever had', he said, 'going over the top on a gee-gee. We had an objective given us two miles away. We had to get there somehow and hold the place until the infantry could get up … and they were shelling us like hell when I copped it'. Mugford's No. 2 – **Lance Corporal Gerald Jones** – was killed almost immediately and Mugford was severely wounded. Ordered to a new position and told to go to the dressing station as soon as it was occupied, he refused to leave his gun and continued to harass the Germans. A shell then broke both his legs and eventually he was taken to a dressing station where he was again wounded in the arm. After treatment involving the amputation of both legs and removal of shrapnel from several parts of his body, he was invalided home and spent two months in hospital in Bedford where, in November 1917, he heard that he had been awarded the VC. Interviewed by the *Bedfordshire Times* on 28 November, he said 'I am the lucky one out of many. I am sure that the others deserved just as much recognition, especially my No. 2, Corporal Jones, who was killed.' Harold Mugford died on 16 June 1958 and was afforded a military funeral in Chelmsford Cathedral. His No. 2 – Gerald George James Jones – has no known grave and is remembered on the Arras Memorial, Bay 10.

Look up the road towards Monchy. It was from that direction that the advanced squadron of 10/Royal Hussars came after they had galloped into the square. **Lieutenant Colonel Hardwick** and his adjutant, **Captain Victor 'Chatty' Greenwood**, were wounded somewhere along here after meeting heavy German machine-gun and artillery fire.

Turn left along the track – which was called **Infantry Lane** by the troops. We are now going to visit the area of Hill 100 – better known as **Infantry Hill** – fought over during the period April–June 1917. **East Trench** – the start line for the attack on Infantry Hill on 14 April 1917 – began here then curved south to cross **Green Lane** 350m away. This is where 1/Essex assembled for the attack with 1/Newfoundland Regiment on their right, south of Green Lane.

Infantry Lane. The electricity pylon marking the beginning of Twin Copses can be seen clearly up ahead.

Continue past a stand of small trees on the left and stop 180m further on. Running off at right angles into the field to your right is the former line of **Shrapnel Trench** which was the German first-line trench on 14 April. It was taken by 1/King's Own Scottish Borderers and 2/South Wales Borderers (29th Division) during the attack of 23 April 1917. If you look across to the left the German line – now **Arrow Trench** – continued on its way to Arrow Head Copse. It was here that D Company of 2/South Wales Borderers lost their two leading officers on 19 May 1917. **Arrow Head Copse** is across to your left and although it still holds its basic shape today, in 1917 it would have been a little more well-defined. **Sergeant Albert White** immediately took command and knocked out an enemy machine-gun post. His posthumous award of the Victoria Cross was gazetted in June of that year.

Continue. Beyond Arrow Head Copse are the **Twin Copses**, behind the electricity pylon in the fields to the left. A further 200m to your right the line of the former **Hill Trench** snakes south. This was the furthest point reached by British forces on 23 April and became the start line for the unsuccessful attack of 3 May.

A little further on Infantry Lane is joined by a track leading to Green Lane, but turn left here and continue gently uphill, for another 90m. This is the approximate point where the former **Hook Trench** ran across the road and represented the furthest point reached in June 1917.

With the **Bois du Vert** on your right, continue uphill to reach **The Mound**, marked by a clump of trees ❽ and a water storage reservoir on the right. If you were to walk on a little further, the village of Boiry-Notre-Dame comes into view. Standing on the summit here it becomes clear just how much of Infantry Hill – known as the *Termitenhügel*, the 'ant hill', on German maps – remained in German hands. Although briefly held by British troops in June 1917, The Mound was never consolidated in 1917 and remained a German strongpoint, finally being captured by Canadian troops in August 1918.

Retrace your route to the junction of tracks and bear left towards Green Lane. ❾ As you do, glance over your shoulder to appreciate the strategic value of The Mound and the importance of the battles for Infantry Hill.

Turn right at the next junction of tracks – this is now Green Lane – and continue for 600m to cross the line of the former **East Trench**. Stop here and turn around to face Infantry Hill. The 1/Newfoundland assembled on your right and attacked on a two-company front.

Looking up the track towards the summit of Infantry Hill. The water storage station can be seen on the right.

Advancing up the hill, the leading companies suffered very heavy casualties from the fire of Bavarian IR 23 before reaching the summit at around 7.00am. Almost immediately the Germans counter-attacked and the surviving Newfoundlanders were surrounded and cut off by the enemy. It was the beginning of a tragedy that ended with the battalion reporting losses of 487 officers and men out of the 591 who had left East Trench at 5.30am. It was a similar story with 1/Essex: having reached The Mound, the battalion was cut off by a swift and 'elastic' German response, with the net result being casualties amounting to over two-thirds of its strength.

Continue along Green Lane to the junction with the main road – Rue de Vis – and stop just before the farmyard on the left. It was in this vicinity **10** that Lieutenant Colonel James Forbes-Robertson, commanding the Newfoundlanders, mobilized his staff and with a small party of men opened targeted fire on the advancing Germans, who by now had counter-attacked and had stumbled across a practically deserted British front line. The private house at the corner of Green Lane and Rue de Vis, 100m further on, is said to be the house from which Forbes-Robertson climbed a ladder to observe the Germans – through a hole blown in the wall – about to occupy East Trench. It was now about 10.45am. Imagine now Forbes-Robertson and nine others dashing the 100m across the open ground to your left from the house to reach a banked hedge line from where they opened fire. They held that position for the next 4 hours. Forbes-Robertson sent Private Albert Rose for reinforcements at 2.00pm and 2/Hampshires arrived 45 minutes later, pushing the Germans back to **Shrapnel Trench**. The action by Forbes-Robertson and his small band undoubtedly saved the day. Collectively they became known as the 'Men who saved Monchy': Forbes-Robertson was awarded the DSO, Captain Kevin Keegan the MC and eight other ranks received the Military Medal. Forbes-Robertson's award of the Victoria Cross a year later, after an action near Vieux-Berquin, came as no surprise to those who knew him.

Lieutenant Colonel James Forbes-Robertson.

Continue to the junction which also marked the position of C Squadron, Essex Yeomanry, on 11 April, whose men were astride Green Lane with machine guns commanding the southeastern approaches to the village.

Turn right at the junction and continue uphill and just before you enter the square you will notice a road – **Rue du Bosquet** – on the right, ⑪ which, in 1917, connected to Infantry Lane. The road now ends amidst rough ground after some 150m. On 11 April one squadron of 10/Royal Hussars was positioned between the road and the D33E – Rue de Pelves – directing fire towards Infantry Lane.

Retrace your route and enter the village square, taking the second road on the left – **Rue de la Chaussy** – to pass the Newfoundland Caribou braying defiantly from the top of a British artillery observation post constructed by 69/Field Company RE in August 1917. ⑫ This road takes you past the church – where you will find the village war memorial and memorials to the Essex battalions and Essex Yeomanry – eventually taking a right-hand fork onto **Rue du Tilleul** to reach the 37th Division Memorial ⑬ situated on the bend in the road. It was on this very corner that the beloved horse of Northamptonshire Yeoman **Trooper Jack Townsend** was hit by machine-gun fire on 11 April as he came around the corner towards you:

I felt, and heard, something strike the inner side of my left field boot, and I looked down expecting that I had been wounded. While I was looking down, Fantail suddenly collapsed on to his knees and his hind legs bent under him. He had been riddled with machine-gun bullets. It was no doubt that it was a spent bullet that had hit my left boot after passing through Fantail's stomach. Luckily for me my horse did not fall until we had reached the cover of the first house beyond the corner. As we went down ... my hands, holding the reins, fell on Fantail's neck. With a loud snorting groan, poor Fantail struggled to rise. Blood sprouted several feet from his nostrils and I became smothered with his gore.

It was said that in several places in Monchy that day the horses were lying so thickly, due to the effects of a German box barrage, that it was necessary to climb over them.

Continue round the bend on Rue du Tilleul to the next crossroads ⑭ where you will see a large *calvaire* and a children's playground ahead of you. To the right of the *calvaire*, incorporated into the private house, are the remains of a German bunker. Whether this is the bunker where **Lieutenant Charles Rutherford** of the Canadian 5/Mounted Rifles encountered a group of Germans on 26 August

The calvaire *where Lieutenant Charles Rutherford came across a large group of German soldiers. Note the former bunker incorporated into the brick wall towards the rear of the house on the right.*

1918 is open to conjecture but his subsequent singlehanded capture of the enemy that day resulted in the award of the Victoria Cross. The road to the right of the *calvaire* was called **Hussar Lane** and is the road along which 8 Cavalry Brigade and the Northamptonshire Yeomanry entered the village from Orange Hill. Should you wish to visit **Orange Trench Cemetery** and **Happy Valley British Cemetery**, you will find them along this road.

Retrace your route to the crossroads. The Essex Yeomanry aid station was in the buildings to the right. It was 'full and overflowing'. This is where medical officer **Captain Ernest Stork** tended the wounded and dying, many of whom had been brought in by men from 111 Brigade. Casualties amongst the Essex Yeomanry were eleven officers and ninety-four other ranks wounded and twenty-seven other ranks killed. Both Stork and **Captain William Wood** received the DSO for their 'conspicuous gallantry' under fire at Monchy.

As you continue along **Rue de la Gaieté** towards the village square, bear in mind that this was the route used by the advanced squadron of the Essex Yeomanry as they entered the village. The sound of horses' hooves on the metalled road would have been heard by the men of 111 Brigade and the defending Germans. Once you have arrived back in the square, walk across to the château gates and stand just inside the grounds looking northeast towards the woods. To your left, A Squadron of the Essex Yeomanry established themselves with two Hotchkiss guns near the wall of the château grounds whilst across to the right, about 150m beyond the red-brick building, was one of Lieutenant Colonel Whitmore's headquarters. Somewhere in the grounds 23-year-old **Lieutenant John Lingeman**, the Essex Yeomanry intelligence officer, was badly wounded whilst trying to get to Whitmore's headquarters with information. Sadly, he died seventeen days later and is buried at Boulogne Eastern Cemetery. On the exterior walls of the *Mairie* you will also find a memorial plaque to **François Delatre**, a local resistance fighter who died in a German concentration camp in 1945.

François Delatre is remembered with a plaque on the wall of the Mairie.

Route 6

Wancourt

Coordinates: 50°14'52.07" N – 2°52'16.77" E
Distance: 8.8km/5.4 miles
Grade: Easy (total ascent 75m)
Suitable for: † ᛈ
Maps: Série Bleue 2406E – Arras and 2506O – Rouvroy/Vitry-en-Artois

General description and context: This is a delightful route which is largely on minor roads and tracks and concentrates on the 23 April 1917 attack by 150 Brigade, although we would recommend visitors familiarize themselves with the sequence of events that took place in the area (see **Route 8**) before exploring the ground above Wancourt.

The physical remains of what was the Wancourt Tower on high ground to the east of the village have now disappeared and although nothing remains today, it is quite obvious where it was situated. Mountain bikers will particularly enjoy the descent down **la Voie du Moulin** and the scenic charm of the riverside road which runs in the valley of the River Cojeul at Guémappe. After a visit to Kestrel Copse and the Hirsch Memorial, we cross the ground over which 150 Brigade attacked before visiting the cluster of CWGC cemeteries east of Héninel. The route returns to Wancourt via Wancourt British Cemetery.

Directions to start: Wancourt is south of Monchy-le-Preux and is best approached using the D33. Park by the church and *Mairie*. ❶

Route description: Life in Wancourt in April 1917 was documented by 20-year-old **Captain John Glubb**, who was serving with 7/Field Company, Royal Engineers. Largely undamaged on 13 April 1917, Glubb recorded that the village was 'pretty well ruined' six days later. Apart from two stores of standard trench materials, the sappers discovered an enormous dump of steel reinforcing bars and concrete, material which Glubb felt had been destined for the further consolidation and strengthening of the Hindenburg Line:

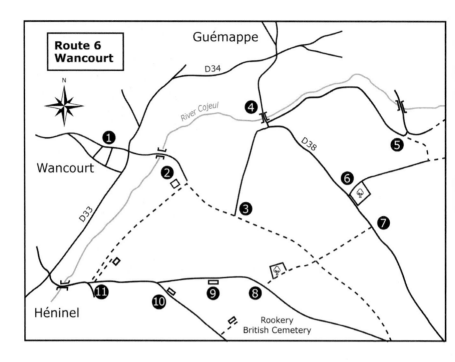

Wancourt contained a great number of mined dugouts, as also did every bank and sunken road in the area. The diligence with which the Germans make mined and concrete dugouts is well known. There was also a good deal of Decauville [manufacturer's name] tramway and derelict trolleys lying about … The Germans also have an excellent scheme for notice boards. Most of the houses round here had white walls on which they painted the name of the village and the direction of the roads. On a wall in Wancourt was a huge notice, which read: 'This road is passable for infantry and artillery between sunrise and sunset, provided no enemy balloon is up'.

The derelict trolleys were obviously part of the German light railway which ran from the former St Rohart Factory on the D939, along the north bank of the Cojeul Valley to Guémappe and on to Wancourt. British plans of the village after its capture confirm Glubb's observations showing at least thirty-one cellars and deep dugouts, three of them in the immediate vicinity of the crossroads near the church where you are parked. Glubb described one such cellar under the ruins of a large house: '[It] must have been used by German officers, for it contained a table, chairs, a piano, and a grandfather clock! Leading down from it was a flight of steps, to a little bedroom dugout fitted with two beds. The sides and top were solid concrete.' As for John Glubb himself, in later life he was known as 'Glubb Pasha', due to his career leading and training Transjordan's Arab Legion between 1939 and 1956. He died in March 1986.

Leave Wancourt on the **Rue d'Alsace** and after crossing the tiny River Cojeul you should be able to see the Cross of Sacrifice of Wancourt British Cemetery another 350m further on. ❷ The ground on which it stands was captured on 12 April 1917 and we suggest you delay your visit until we return here later in the route.

Sir John Bagot Glubb, photographed in the 1950s while in command of the Arab League.

From the cemetery continue uphill on a track passing a wind turbine on the right. After 470m you will reach a metalled single-track road on the left. Stop here. According to trench maps and old aerial photographs the **Wancourt Tower** – a former windmill – was in the field on the right: continue the line of the road coming in from your left into the field for about 70m. ❸ The tower was captured on 16 April by 6/Northumberland Fusiliers but on the night of 17 April the Germans temporarily wrested back control before 7/Northumberland Fusiliers, 'advanced in perfect order and with little opposition retook the tower and the neighbouring trenches'. Captain John Glubb's company of sappers was ordered to demolish the tower:

> The building, which was known as the Wancourt Tower, was found to contain a solid concrete machine-gun emplacement, the gun from which had caused us heavy losses. The Fusiliers were holding a line just this side of the building, the Boche a hundred yards beyond it … The infantry said it was impossible to get there by day, the whole hillside being as bare as a plate. Littlewood, however, walked straight up the hill and into the

emplacement at two o'clock in the afternoon! He measured up the whole place and walked back again.

Taking a party of sappers with him, 19-year-old **Second Lieutenant Charles Littlewood** returned and demolished the tower without a shot being fired! Glubb wrote that he was furious that they had demolished the tower without a single weapon between them but the story still ranks as one of the more humorous aspects of what was a bloody and costly battle. Littlewood was killed by shellfire in July 1917 and is buried in London Cemetery, Neuville-Vitasse.

On 23 April 1917, 150 Brigade – 50th (Northumbrian) Division – attacked from here towards **Kestrel Copse** and Chérisy. On its left was 44 Brigade – 15th (Scottish) Division – and, on the right, 90 Brigade of the 30th Division. The attack cost 4/East Yorkshires 363 officers and men killed, missing and wounded. **Captain Cecil Slack**, who was acting adjutant of the battalion at the time, wrote that they were the first to reach their objective but were cut off by a German counter-attack on the left flank.

Turn left onto the minor road – appropriately called **la Voie du Moulin** – which runs downhill towards **Guémappe**. There are excellent views of Monchy-le-Preux dominating the skyline up

The road leading down to Guémappe from the high ground above Wancourt. The village of Guémappe is in the foreground with Monchy-le-Preux on the skyline.

ahead – it is clear from here why Monchy was such 'vital ground' – and as you near Guémappe, **Tank Cemetery** and the D939 can also be seen. Follow the road down through the bends to reach a small bridge spanning the River Cojeul. ❹ Guémappe was initially taken by 44 Brigade but after 2/Seaforths were pushed out of the village by a German counter-attack it was left to 46 Brigade to finally secure it on 26 April. In the meantime, the Germans were able to direct heavy machine-gun fire into the left flank of 150 Brigade as they advanced towards Kestrel Copse.

Take the track which runs alongside the River Cojeul, marked by the regular line of tall trees to the left. Follow the river for about 700m before veering right across fields towards a long stretch of woodland. German gun batteries and gun pits were dug in alongside the D38 and the slope to your right before 9 April 1917. Note that if you had been traversing this route at about 4.50am on 23 April you would have been under very heavy artillery fire as this whole area was being plastered with German 105mm and 150mm shells. On reaching the wood after another 700m you will come to a junction of tracks with a track on your right running uphill through the trees. ❺ Take this track – it soon opens out to run along the rough line of **Ape Support Trench**, just 150m behind what was British front line

The D38 can be seen on the right with the minor road running alongside the River Cojeul on the left.

of 21 March 1918 – to meet a T-junction after 300m. A right turn here will take you to **Kestrel Copse**. Stop at the **Hirsch Memorial**. **6**

The 1/4 Yorkshire Regiment war diary tells us that on 23 April 1917 W Company passed the German first-line trenches with the aid of a tank before the battalion moved on to capture the German support line. Heavy fire had reduced the battalion's numbers and it was 'by now considerably thinned out'; 20-year-old Leeds-born **Captain David Philip 'Pip' Hirsch** found himself the only officer left with Y Company. Establishing a defensive flank with half of Y Company, at about 6.00am he dug them in on a line 'above and parallel to the river [and] with the remainder of the battalion (about 150 men) he decided to hold on to this position and sent back for reinforcements and [ammunition]'. That flank was right of, and parallel to, the track you have just come up. Hirsch had no contact with 4/East Yorkshires, who should have been on his right, as that battalion had lost all its officers earlier in the attack. To all intents and purposes he was surrounded on three sides. Twice wounded in the engagement, Hirsch was eventually killed around 7.15am and his posthumous Victoria Cross was gazetted in June 1917. His body was lost after the war and he is commemorated on the Arras

The Hirsch Memorial.

Memorial, but the granite memorial that you see today is the result of the generosity of the inhabitants of Guémappe and was officially unveiled in April 2017. The British front line eventually stabilized east of the copse.

Before you leave, note that it was somewhere on this ground – straddling the road towards Guémappe, between the copse and the River Cojeul – that Second Lieutenant Charles Littlewood, the 19-year-old Royal Engineer who was responsible for the demolition of the Wancourt Tower, was killed on 10 July 1917 'by a stray shell, field gun when walking across the open from SHIKAR to KESTREL AVENUES by night'.

From Kestrel Copse turn left towards Chérisy for 340m then take the track on the right. ❼ Continue for 600m to a junction of tracks and go straight over towards **Sablonnières Copse** which you can see ahead of you on the right. At the junction with the road turn right. ❽ The copse which has grown up on the junction now hides a former quarry, although in 1917 both copses were non-existent. The road now goes gently uphill to **Bootham Cemetery** which soon comes into view on the left. ❾ After leaving the cemetery continue uphill to the junction where CWGC signs point the way to **Chérisy Road East**

Bootham Cemetery.

A small brick-built chapel by the side of the road marks the start of two tracks; the one on the left leads cross country to Wancourt, while that on the right leads to Héninel Communal Cemetery Extension.

Cemetery (see **Route 8**). ⑩ Retrace your route from the cemetery and turn left and halfway down the hill to Héninel you will see a small, brick-built chapel on the right where two tracks are apparent. We are going to follow the track signposted Héninel Communal Cemetery Extension, which has a line of trees on its left. ⑪

Héninel Communal Cemetery Extension
Héninel was captured in a snowstorm on 12 April 1917 by the 56th (London) Division along with elements of the 21st Division and the 50th (Northumbrian) Division. The cemetery was opened by the 50th Division a short time later. On 23 April the division took part in the attack from the vicinity of the Wancourt Tower towards Chérisy, in which 4/East Yorkshires were involved and, although most of the division's battalions are represented here, there are no casualties from 4/East Yorkshires for that day. Today there are 140 burials in the cemetery, of which seven are unidentified. Of the seven men killed on 23 April, three are from 5/Yorkshire, a battalion that was advancing with 4/East Yorkshires. All three were men with young families; 29-year-old **Private Charles Frow** (D.1) was a grocer's assistant when he enlisted in Doncaster and lived in Bridlington with his wife Harriet. Buried next to him is 38-year-old **Private Robert**

Héninel Communal Cemetery Extension.

Moore (D.2), who enlisted in Scarborough and lived in the town with his wife Florrie and two children. **Private Frederick Diaper** (B.8), aged 30, enlisted in Norwich and lived in Swaffham with his wife and two children. The names of these three men, almost anonymous amongst myriad others, emphasize the fact that each headstone has a story to tell and the man buried beneath was little different to you or I. Decorated for gallantry was 32-year-old **Captain Hugh Longbourne** (B.17), who was killed by a sniper on 3 May 1917. Serving with 7/Queen's Royal West Surreys, he was awarded the DSO in 1916 for capturing a machine gun and taking forty-six prisoners at the Schwaben Redoubt near Thiepval on the Somme on 28 September. His brother, Brigadier General Francis Longbourne, also won the DSO and went on to command 171 Brigade during the last year of the war. An individual who volunteered for service late in life was 36-year-old **Lieutenant William Poole** (E.13), who was killed serving with 5/Northumberland Fusiliers on 19 September 1917. Born in Scarborough the third son of schoolmaster and, later, ordained George Poole – who died in February 1917 – and his wife Clara, he followed his father to University College, Durham, where he matriculated as an arts student in the Michaelmas term of 1902. He only attended for a year.

William Poole was gazetted as a second lieutenant in August 1915 and lieutenant on 1 July 1917 – albeit not officially notified until November. Between 17 and 20 September 1917 5/Northumberland Fusiliers were in the front line under heavy shell and mortar fire shortly after relieving 4/Northumberland Fusiliers some 550m east of Kestrel Copse. On 19 and 20 September patrols were sent out into no-man's-land to investigate German working parties. William Poole was killed either as a result of shellfire or whilst on patrol – the war diary is not specific. His name also appears on a memorial plaque in Christ Church parish church, Walker, Newcastle upon Tyne – its former location was the 5/Northumberland Fusiliers' Drill Hall at Walker. He is also remembered on Durham University's Roll of Service.

From the cemetery you can either return to the road to take the lower of the two tracks or, for the more energetic, scramble down the bank with care at an appropriate point. At the junction of tracks beyond the cemetery go straight ahead. You may now catch a glimpse of the River Cojeul on your left as it runs parallel to the track, skirting the eastern side of Wancourt. It was this small river that we crossed by the bridge south of Guémappe.

For the last 500m the track runs almost alongside the former **Kestrel Avenue** support trench, taking us to the entrance of **Wancourt British Cemetery**, the details of which can be found in **Route 8**. ❷ From the cemetery turn left at the junction with the road and cross the River Cojeul to return to your vehicle in Wancourt but before you do, a short detour of 250m or so along the field edge on the far, Wancourt bank of the Cojeul will take you to a British concrete shelter built after the British occupation. In his *Armageddon's Walls-British Pill Boxes 1914–1918*, Peter Oldham noted that it was not particularly strong, being built at a time when the RE were under constant bombardment. The roof – now collapsed – perhaps consisted of the German steel girders found in Wancourt after its capture by John Glubb and his engineers. Another 50m further will take you to a German bunker with very thick, shell-proof walls and roof, which was constructed with care and at leisure, several kilometres behind the then front line. The contemporary British plan of Wancourt, drawn after 9 April 1917, recorded this bunker and its position in relation to the area near the church: 'Concrete redoubt, 50 men, 200yds away near river'. It is interesting to note that these two bunkers also mark the furthest extent of the German spring offensive of 1918. During the following months they were in the German front line, with the British line only 100m or so to the west. The damage could have occurred during this period.

Route 7

Bullecourt

Coordinates: 50°11′34.16″ N – 2°55′46.96″ E
Distance: 7.3km/4.5 miles
Grade: Easy (total ascent 46m)
Suitable for: ⫯ ♿
Maps: Série Bleue 2506O – Rouvroy/Vitry-en-Artois

General description and context: This is a complex battlefield, largely due to the number of units involved and the length of time it took to capture Bullecourt. There were two battles at Bullecourt in 1917: three if you count the assault on the **'Red Patch'** on 12 May. Whilst we have provided an overview of the fighting in **Route 8**, our route here focuses on the eastern flank. The Australians referred to the two trench systems of the Hindenburg Line as 'OG1' and 'OG2', terms derived from their experience after capturing two German trench lines at Pozières which they encountered in 1916 and, which, for ease of reference, we have adopted.

The first attack on the village coincided with a snowstorm and was intended to begin on 10 April, but the failure of the tanks of D Battalion to arrive on time led to the cancellation of the Australian attack, although the battalions of 185 Brigade, which had not received the cancellation order, suffered 162 dead, the majority being from 2/7 West Yorkshires. It was not an auspicious start to Sir Hubert Gough's Fifth Army assault.

On 11 April the 4th Australian Division attacked on the eastern side of Bullecourt with 12 Brigade on the left of **Central Road** and 4 Brigade to the right with the additional objective of Riencourt lès Cagnicourt. The whole attack was supported by twelve tanks of which only eleven made it to the start line and they proved largely ineffective. On the left flank was 185 Brigade – 62nd (West Riding) Division – tasked with advancing only when the Australians and the tanks had entered Bullecourt. It was a disaster and although Australian troops entered both the German front line (OG1) and OG2, they were unable to consolidate their advance and were pushed back to their start line by the tenacious defence of the **27th (Württemberg) Division**.

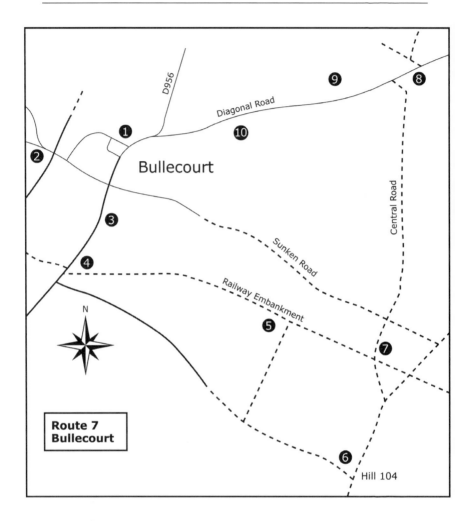

Observing no Australian troops or tanks in the village, 185 Brigade remained in situ and did not attack. It must be said the tank support was largely ineffective and failed in its task of crushing the enormous belts of wire that protected the Hindenburg Line.

On 3 May the Australian 4th Division attacked with 5 and 6 brigades on either side of Central Road. Tanks again supported the attack but on this occasion they were deployed with the 62nd Division, which was attacking in front and to the left of Bullecourt with all three of its brigades. Leading the Australian 5 Brigade attack to the right of Central Road, 17/ and 19/Battalions managed to reach OG1 but were turned back by severe machine-gun fire from

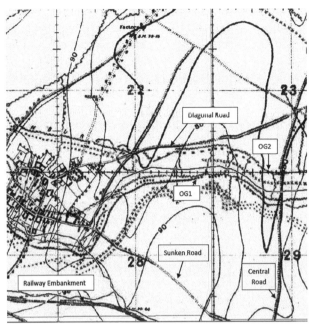

A trench map showing the Hindenburg Line around Bullecourt and the eastern flank assaulted by the Australians.

OG1 and **Balcony Trench** on the Quéant Ridge. The 6 Brigade gained OG1 and then took OG2 at 4.40am, with a party under **Captain Gordon Maxfield** reaching the **Six Crossroads** an hour later. The men of 185 Brigade gained OG1 and pushed into the village, whilst on the left flank, men of 186 Brigade established themselves on the far side of the village near a sugar factory and at one point they were less than 1,000m west of Maxfield and his men. Unfortunately, neither group could see the other. The tanks were a little more effective than they had been on 11 April but by midday the battle was lost; 2/5 West Yorkshires had been expelled from the village and only 100 men from 2/6 West Yorkshires returned to their trenches. The 62nd Division had lost a total of

The Church of St-Vaast.

116 officers and 2,860 other ranks. The only success of the day was the 6 Australian Brigade which retained control of its ground until relieved by 1 Brigade at 1.00am on 4 May. The penultimate German counter-attack was launched on the morning of 6 May against the Australian 11/ and 12/Battalions, which was stopped on Central Road by 24-year-old **Corporal George 'Snowy' Howell**, 1/Battalion, running alongside OG1 and throwing grenades into the trench until he was wounded. His award of the Victoria Cross was gazetted in June 1917. With the Germans now north of OG2 and much of the village in Allied hands, all that remained was to clear the troublesome **Red Patch** in the south of the village.

Our route begins by the church in Bullecourt **❶** visiting the **Crucifix** and the Red Patch to pass the water tower on the way to the former railway embankment. We make a short visit to **Hill 104** before returning to **Central Road** and the site of **Six Crossroads**, where much of the fighting on this flank took place. From here we return to Bullecourt along **Diagonal Road** passing the Missing in Action and Digger Memorials. You will find photographs of these and other memorials in Bullecourt in **Route 8**.

Directions to start: Bullecourt is best approached from Arras along the D5 and D956. Park by the Church of St-Vaast opposite the *Mairie*.

The Mairie, *opposite the church.*

Route Description: Before you leave the vicinity of the church, see if the *Mairie* is open and view the painting by James Scott, depicting the death of **Major Percy Black**, commanding 16/Australian Battalion, on 11 May. However, opening times appear to be erratic and it may be advisable to email the *Mairie* in advance: mairie.bullecourt@wanadoo.fr. With your back to the church take the minor road opposite – Rue de l'Ecole – to the right of the *Mairie* and follow the road through a sharp left-hand bend to a T-junction. Turn right for 90m to reach the **Crucifix**. ❷ In May 1917 the area around the Crucifix was the site of the rather precarious German lifeline along which reinforcements and supplies were brought into the Red Patch, so-called because it was coloured red on trench maps. The Red Patch was the last remaining enemy stronghold in the southwest corner of Bullecourt and was stubbornly defended by the **German Guards Fusiliers** and as long as the vital corridor to the Hindenburg Line was kept open at the Crucifix, the Red Patch could be reinforced.

At 3.40am on 12 May 1917, 91 Brigade (7th Division) was tasked with capturing the Red Patch and linking up with the 15 Australian Brigade (5th Australian Division) whilst to the hapless 185 Brigade of 62nd Division fell the unenviable task of overwhelming the Crucifix. The 91 Brigade got off to a good start and advanced quickly to reach

The crucifix stands between two substantial conifers.

the ruins of the church to link up with 2/Queen's and the men of the 15 Australian Brigade, who had bombed their way along OG2 towards them. During this attack 21-year-old **Lieutenant Rupert Moon** of 58/Australian Battalion – already wounded in the face and shoulder – surged forward and with a cry of 'Come on, you'll not see me left boys' rallied his men to capture a strongpoint. He was awarded the Victoria Cross. Despite this advance, 185 Brigade failed to take the Crucifix leaving the Red Patch and its corridor intact. A renewed assault was made at 2.10am on 14 May by 1/Royal Welsh Fusiliers of 22 Brigade, which very nearly succeeded before the ground was again lost to an enemy counter-attack. It was finally left to two brigades of the 58th Division to take this stronghold on 17 May, and after a short bombardment,

The water tower on the D956.

The narrow entrance to the line of the former railway on the D956.

they cleared through and captured the utterly devastated village.

With the Crucifix behind you continue straight ahead along **Rue d'Arras** to find the Bullecourt Museum on your left. We suggest you delay your visit until you have completed the route but be aware of the opening times. The Rue d'Arras represents the centre line of the former Red Patch which, according to the 7th Division's historian, 'was alive with Germans'. It was in this area that a party of 2/Honourable Artillery Company (22 Brigade) under **Corporal Reginald Billingham** was found on 7 May still holding out in the ruins, having been left behind on 3 May.

Lieutenant Tom Armistead.

At the junction with the D956 turn right and after approximately 130m stop. This is where the first line trench – **Tower Trench** – of the protective Hindenburg Line crossed the road before it enveloped the village to

The track along the former railway embankment.

the west – towards the Crucifix – and to the east. Continue past the water tower ❸ and take the narrow grass track on the left, ❹ which is part of the Australian Trail. The track takes you onto the line of the former Boisleux–Marquion railway and it was this initial section that was the start line for 2/6 West Yorkshires during Second Bullecourt. One of the men killed in this assault was 22-year-old **Lieutenant Tom Armistead**, commanding C Company. The battalion was tasked with linking up with the Australians, and Armistead's company managed to get into the outskirts of the village before he was killed whilst overwhelming a German machine-gun position. Already the holder of the MC, he is commemorated on the Arras Memorial.

The track soon becomes an embankment and it takes little imagination to see the protection offered by the southern aspect of this feature.

After 500m the track begins to bend to the right and the sunken road, marked by a hedge, comes into view on the left, stop here. At 3.45am on 3 May the Australian 26/Battalion was in position along the railway line and 21/ and 22/Battalions were deployed between the embankment and the Sunken Road. The fighting strength of 22/Battalion was twenty-one officers and 618 other ranks, **Captain Eugene Gorman**, the battalion historian, described their reception:

> Given the position of the battalion on the left of 6 Brigade it had the task of advancing at almost point blank range to the Germans garrisoning the eastern side of Bullecourt, and as a result caused its casualties to exceed those of any other [Australian] battalion

The track leading up to Hill 104, the crest of which is to the left of the photograph. The church spire is that of Noreuil.

engaged on that day … The intensity of the machine-gun fire
was not equalled in any of the 22/Battalion's other experiences
during the war.

Gorman's service with 22/Battalion at Bullecourt resulted in his
award of the MC. Despite the staggering casualties and those of
21/Battalion following on behind, the Australians reached OG1 and
advanced into OG2. Within the first 2 hours of the attack 6 Brigade
had established itself in both trench systems of the Hindenburg
Line. During the course of 24 hours 22/Battalion lost sixteen officers
and 422 other ranks out of the twenty-one and 618 who had gone
into battle; 50 per cent were either killed or missing. CWGC records
indicate that 165 were killed or died of wounds. In total the Australian
6 Brigade lost fifty-eight officers and 1,422 other ranks.

On a clear day you should be able to see the **Digger Memorial**
across to the left, marked by the two flagpoles, situated between
OG1 and OG2.

Continue along the embankment turning right at the next track **5**
towards Noreuil. This follows the rough line of a later trench known
as **Tank Avenue** and after 600m you will reach a T-junction where
a left turn will take you up towards Hill 104. **6** It was here that
Second Lieutenant David Morris abandoned his tank D/25, No. 711
on 11 April after developing clutch trouble. On the extreme right
of the attack Morris's tank and that of **Second Lieutenant Harold
Puttock** (D/24, No. 593) had moved forward but both had come
under 'tremendous machine-gun fire' in front of the German wire.

The sunken road with Bullecourt in the distance.

Both withdrew towards the railway where Puttock's tank was hit and disabled. Morris succeeded in towing **Second Lieutenant Hugh Skinner's** tank (D/23, No. 796) over the railway embankment before crawling back up this track towards Noreuil with his machine's clutch slipping. The tank broke down and was then hit and knocked out. Morris took part in the Third Battle of Ypres and the Cambrai tank attack seven months later. He survived the war.

After taking in the sweeping views – on a clear day – from Hill 104 turn left to follow the track downhill towards the railway embankment. At the obvious fork – named **Sydney Cross** on trench maps – bear left along the grass track and return to the line of the embankment. ❼ This is where **Brigadier John Gelibrand**, commanding 6 Brigade, had his headquarters for Second Bullecourt. Go straight across onto **Central Road** and stop after 200m at the crossroads. To your left is the **Sunken Road** where on the night of 10 April **Captain Albert Jacka**, 14/Battalion, together with two officers from 16/Battalion, crawled towards the German lines to ascertain the damage caused to the wire and the strength of the opposition. Reporting that the wire had not been sufficiently damaged, the reply astounded the Australians: there was to be no opening artillery barrage and the tanks, which would not operate with artillery, would crush the wire. The Australian experience with the tanks was woeful and mistrust of their worth ran deep. **Sergeant Edgar Rule**, serving with C Company, 14/Battalion, was singularly unimpressed with their performance:

> A tank directly in front of me was stuck in a shell hole, and its crew were tinkering around it. Later another tank came to its assistance, but it seemed to me that it should have supported our troops instead of attending to other business in the back area. A third was between Bullecourt and Riencourt, and, as I watched, it started to move towards the Hun wire. On reaching the wire, it burst out in flames – apparently no man escaped, for I saw none leave it. Another was retiring when a shell burst at its side. The crew jumped out, one at a time, and ran to shelter. Several others were burning fiercely, belching out dense clouds of black smoke, and they continued to burn for hours.

Australian faith in the value of armour would not be restored until the stunningly successful Battle of Hamel east of Amiens on 4 July 1918.

From the Sunken Road, the open ground to the right of Central Road was the ground over which the 4 Brigade battalions attacked.

Lieutenant Thomas Chataway, 15/Battalion, described the opening moments of the advance:

> At 4.47am the 15th Battalion deployed into artillery formation and, under heavy fire, followed in the wake of the 14th Battalion, through which it ultimately had to pass. Of the six tanks allotted to the 4th Brigade for the attack, only three were in position. These moved forward at 4.40am. Across the expanse of snow moved the four lines of the leading battalions, the 14th on the left and the 16th on the right, keeping perfect distance and stepping out as if on parade … The [German] machine gunners, their targets now visible, poured a deadly crossfire into the advancing men. Leaving the tanks behind and pressing forward the 14th and 16th Battalions came to the wire entanglements.

Ordered to wait until the tanks had passed, the two battalions of 12 Brigade left their start line long after 4 Brigade had advanced but, despite the late arrival of the tanks and the onset of daylight, 46/Battalion got into OG1 and 48/Battalion into OG2.

As you continue towards Riencourt the church spire comes into view, as does **Diagonal Road** which marks the approximate line of OG2 and the approximate line of the final Australian advance. A glance behind you will reveal the line of the railway embankment marked by the line of trees. A little under 800m from the Sunken Road is where OG1 crossed Central Road, a distance that illustrates the length of the advance undertaken on 11 April. It was in this area that **Corporal Howell** won the Victoria Cross on 12 May. Ponder for a moment Thomas Chataway's description as 15/Battalion reached the wire:

> They were raked unmercifully by machine guns that swept them again and again off their feet. At least 100 of the battalion

Corporal George Howell.

fell when moving along the wire seeking the entrances or when passing through them. The now sadly depleted 15th joined up with the 14th, and the two battalions leapt with fury at the second belt of wire, and hacking and slashing their way through, secured a footing in the second objective.

Across to the right of Central Road **Major Percy Black** was leading the right flank of 16/Battalion which was exposed to uncut wire and machine-gun fire at OG1 after the tanks had failed to arrive. Charging forward, he is said to have yelled 'Come on boys, bugger the tanks!' and was shot through the head leading his men through the wire. He is commemorated on the Villers-Bretonneux Memorial.

Continue along Central Road to where the track takes a sharp bend to the left to meet Diagonal Road. At the T-junction with the road turn right and after 170m you will come to the site of the former Six Crossroads. **❽** There are only four roads remaining today and the site of Captain George Maxwell's advanced post, which he established on 3 May, is in the fields to the left of Diagonal Road. He is commemorated on the Villers-Bretonneux Memorial too.

Retrace your route past the track leading to Central Road and continue towards Bullecourt. The **Cross Memorial ❾** is another 450m along the road and whilst you are there you will notice one plaque dedicated to Percy Black. The area in which **Lieutenant Rupert Moon** won his Victoria Cross is in the fields across the road.

Continue to the Australian Memorial Park **❿** and the Digger Memorial. The park was constructed between the two trench lines of the Hindenburg Line and is dedicated to the thousands of Australians killed and wounded in the battles of Bullecourt. Both these monuments are described in **Route 8**. Walk to the rear of the park and look back across the fields to the line of the railway. In November 1994, a local farmer ploughing his field behind the park found the remains of **Sergeant John White** of 22/Battalion, along with a wallet containing fragments of a letter and a lock of hair. White's identity disc

Major Percy Black.

was still intact. He was buried a year later in Quéant Road Cemetery in the presence of his daughter, Myrtle Prophet, then 81 years old.

Just after leaving the Digger Memorial a track on the right marks the point at which OG2 left the road and continued behind the village.

Continue to the church, which, like the remainder of the village, was reduced to rubble. Before you head for the nearby **Canberra Café**, bear in mind you are still in the centre of the battlefield. This was the point reached by a party of 2/5 West Yorkshires on 3

Lieutenant Rupert Moon.

May 1917, a feat repeated on 12 May by a party from 1/South Staffs (91 Brigade) which finally made contact with men of 2/Queen's who had advanced on the right flank. It was the beginning of the end of a battle that had raged since 10 April 1917.

Bullecourt fell again into German hands on 21 March 1918 and was re-captured for the last time on 21 August 1918 by the London Scottish.

Route 8

Southern Car Tour

Coordinates: 50°17′43.18″ N – 2°50′01.50″ E
Distance: 43.5km/27 miles
Suitable for: 🚗
Maps: Série Bleue 2406E – Arras, 2407E – Bapaume, 2506O – Rouvroy/
Vitry-en-Artois and 2507O – Croisilles

General description and context: This is a linear tour that begins at the car park adjoining Feuchy Communal Cemetery and concludes at London Cemetery on the D5, northwest of Neuville-Vitasse. After travelling along the Scarpe we turn south through Roeux and to Monchy-le-Preux before looking briefly at the actions around Guémappe, Wancourt, Héninel and Chérisy. We then make our way to Bullecourt, the scene of the Fifth Army attacks on the Hindenburg Line, before heading through Écoust-St-Mein and Croisilles. After passing under the A1 Autoroute and railway line, we visit Henin-sur-Cojeul and Neuville-Vitasse before concluding the route opposite Telegraph Hill.

Directions to start: Feuchy is best approached from the D42 from Arras. After reaching the crossroads at Athies (Athies Communal Cemetery on the left) turn right towards the railway line to find the Feuchy Communal Cemetery on the D258.

Route description: Proceed alongside the boundary of Feuchy Communal Cemetery – there are no British and Commonwealth casualties here – to the railway bridge which you will see on your right. This railway line comes from Arras and passes through Railway Triangle as it continues towards Douai. This is **Spider Corner** and on the far side of the archway a minor road and track leads down **Battery Valley** on Chemin des Fonds and to **Houdain Lane Cemetery** along Chemin des Revers (see **Route 2**). Follow the road round to the left, noting the grass track on the right – Rue du Petit Bois – leading uphill towards the Feuchy Redoubt.

The railway bridge at Spider Corner.

Feuchy and the 1914 Battles on the Scarpe

The battle for Arras began on 2 October 1914 with the defence of the town entrusted to **Général Louis de Maud'huy** and the French Tenth Army. However, far from encountering the expected feeble cavalry screen, the French found themselves confronted by three German Corps which pushed them back leaving only **Général Ernest Barbot's 77th Division** stubbornly holding their positions at Feuchy. The next two days brought more French reverses as the Germans occupied Lens and menaced the southern outskirts of Arras. Still fighting at Feuchy, Ernest Barbot, realizing he was in danger of being encircled, withdrew further west into the outskirts of St-Laurent-Blangy. On 22 October the Belfry Tower on the magnificent Hôtel de Ville was destroyed and the Germans attacked the eastern outskirts of St-Laurent-Blangy. Incredibly, the Germans were held along the line that was to become the jumping off point for the British 1917 offensive. Barbot had effectively saved Arras. The Barbot Memorial is featured in our companion guidebook *Arras North*.

In 1917 Feuchy was taken by the 15th (Scottish) Division on the opening day of the Arras offensive, but before the village could be taken the **Feuchy Redoubt** had to be overcome (see **Route 1**). In an attempt to outflank the redoubt, units of 46 Brigade took **Observation Ridge** and continued their advance into the northern end of **Battery Valley** – known by the Germans as *Artillerie Mulde* – allowing 44 Brigade to advance parallel with the railway line. In the end it was a Mark II Tank called *Lusitania*, commanded by **Second Lieutenant Charles Weber**, that advanced along the railway line from the Railway Triangle east of Arras and 'persuaded' the German garrison in the redoubt to relocate to a dugout near Spider Corner, from which they were flushed out. The village was taken by 7/KOSB and two companies from 10/Scottish Rifles, but was again in German hands after the March 1918 offensive. It was finally retaken in August 1918 by 152 Brigade, 51st (Highland) Division.

At the junction with the D258 turn right to the roundabout where a right turn along the D37 Rue d'Athies, signposted Feuchy Centre, will take you to another roundabout and Feuchy British Cemetery. On reaching the roundabout the entrance to the cemetery is almost straight ahead and you will find a handy car park to the left of the church hall.

Feuchy British Cemetery

The cemetery was begun by the 12th (Eastern) Division and used until March 1918. In 1926 Plot I, which now backs onto the railway line, was realigned to make way for a railway station. The cemetery now contains 209 casualties, five of whom are unidentified, along with two special memorials. Almost half the burials here are gunners and date from April and May 1917 when the Battle of Arras was taking place. One of these was 24-year-old **Second Lieutenant William Shand-Kydd** (II.E.9) serving with A Battery, 51 Brigade, Royal Field Artillery when he was killed on 19 May 1917. Shand-Kydd originally came from Arbroath in Scotland but after the war his two younger brothers, Norman and Rowland, moved to London where they developed the well-known wallpaper manufacturing business in Highgate. Norman had a son Peter who married Frances, the late Diana, the Princess of Wales's mother, after she divorced her first husband – and Diana's father – the 8th Earl Spencer.

If you want to find a grave on which to place your cross of remembrance look no further than 21-year-old **Sapper Alfred Allen** (II.B.11), who was killed on 8 May 1917 whilst serving with 87/Field Company, Royal Engineers. An apprentice wheelwright before he

Feuchy British Cemetery.

The Mairie *and village war memorial in Feuchy.*

enlisted in January 1916, he arrived in France at the beginning of October 1916 and served on the Somme before meeting his death at Arras. He is also commemorated on the village memorial and in St Peter's Church at Empingham.

Return to the roundabout taking the first exit towards the *Mairie* and war memorial along **Rue des Acacias**. Turn right at the junction along **Rue de Fampoux** and continue for 2km to a junction where a left turn will take you over the River Scarpe. At the stop sign go straight across and continue uphill, across a mini roundabout, to the junction with the D42. Turn right and in 100m you will see the entrance to Fampoux Communal Cemetery opposite the church and next to the war memorial.

Fampoux was captured by the men of 2/Duke of Wellington's at 4.40pm on 9 April 1917 and remained behind the Allied front line until the German offensive of March 1918. The town was finally cleared by the 51st (Highland) Division as they advanced along the Scarpe on 26 August 1918.

Fampoux Communal Cemetery
There is parking outside the cemetery entrance. The casualties here are all from the Second World War and the British plot is to the right of the main entrance. Of the ten casualties buried here, only four are identified and, of these, three men are from 4/Green Howards who were fighting in the village in the second half of May 1940.

Leave the cemetery and continue uphill, along what was **Border Lane**, bearing right at the junction, to find the Seaforth Highlanders' Memorial on the right. This was known to the British as **Northumberland Lane** and it is probably better to continue for another 120m to reach **Sunken Road Cemetery**, where you can turn round after your visit, stopping by the Seaforths' Memorial on the way downhill.

Sunken Road Cemetery and the Seaforth Highlanders' Memorial
It is strange that the cemetery contains none of the men of 10 Brigade who made the attack towards Roeux on 11 April 1917, nor, it would seem, are there any casualties from the attack on the **Hyderabad Redoubt**, which was some 320m to the east of the cemetery. The

Redoubt was taken on 9 April by 1/Rifle Brigade, some of whom reportedly followed a football kicked by **Corporal Bancroft** into the enemy trenches. The battalion war diary records the capture of the redoubt:

> The redoubt was occupied at about 4.30pm and by 3.00am on April 10th the situation was fairly secure and touch had been gained with the 12th Brigade on the right. During the 9th a total of 10 officers – including a general and his staff – and thirteen other ranks had been captured, also three heavy howitzers, a travelling kitchen, a machine gun and much telephone equipment and a mass of official documents, orders and maps.

There are good views from the rear wall of the cemetery towards the ground formerly occupied by the Hyderabad Redoubt.

Border Lane achieved notoriety on 11 April 1917 when two battalions from 10 Brigade – **2/Seaforth Highlanders** and **1/Royal Irish Fusiliers** – attacked the German line in the fields beyond the cemetery at midday. The objective allotted to the Seaforths ran from the château south of the Chemical Works at Roeux to a crossroads now buried under the intersection of the A1 and A26 Autoroutes. Having already been spotted by the Germans whilst forming up, the Seaforths advanced across more than a kilometre of largely open ground under a hail of machine-gun fire directed from the railway embankment and the Chemical Works at Roeux. It was a disaster: over 90 per cent of the battalion were either killed or wounded; only fifty-seven men survived intact. Leading a party of Seaforths was 21-year-old **Lieutenant Donald Mackintosh** who almost succeeded in reaching the railway station at Roeux. Wounded in the leg, he and his diminishing band of men held off repeated German counter-attacks until they were finally overcome. For his gallantry Mackintosh was awarded the Victoria Cross and his body and many of his comrades lie in **Brown's Copse Cemetery** on the

The Seaforth Highlanders' Memorial.

outskirts of Roeux (see **Route 3**). If you stand with your back to the memorial looking east across the open farmland, try to imagine the scene of carnage in front of you; dead and dying men lying on the battlefield with some of the wounded struggling to get back to the safety of the sunken lane where you are standing. The 10 Brigade war diary later reported that 'there could be seen a long row of dead Seaforth Highlanders cut down like grass by machine gun fire'.

Second Lieutenant Bernard Cassidy.

On 28 March 1918, the ground 700m to the northwest – the Fampoux Ridge – was the scene of the stand of 2/Lancashire Fusiliers when the Germans launched Operation *Mars* on both banks of the Scarpe, with the intention of capturing Arras and Vimy Ridge. By 9.00am 2/Essex, in the front line, had been overwhelmed but the German onslaught was eventually held by the Lancashire Fusiliers. Amongst the dead was **Second Lieutenant Bernard Cassidy**, commanding A Company, who had been ordered to hold the ground at all costs. Running short of ammunition, Cassidy and his men were surrounded and he was killed, his actions resulting in a posthumous Victoria Cross. He is commemorated on the Arras Memorial.

From the memorial retrace your route and bear left at the fork, downhill to Fampoux and the junction with the D42. Turn left – signposted Roeux and Plouvain – passing underneath the power lines to reach a bridge over the railway and A1 Autoroute. At the next crossroads turn right onto the D33, signposted Monchy-le-Preux. After 185m you will cross over the railway line to see a supermarket on the left. Stop here.

The Roeux Chemical Works

You are now on the site of the former Chemical Works, which was in reality a derelict dye factory and was the object of the 10 Brigade attack on 11 April 1917. The following day two brigades from the 9th (Scottish) Division attacked across the same ground with an

The railway station at Roeux. A supermarket has been built behind and to the right on the site of the former Chemical Works.

outcome that mirrored the 10 Brigade attack, the *Official History* citing a hurried preparation, inadequate reconnaissance and an ineffective artillery bombardment for the failure. **Lieutenant Richard Talbot-Kelly**, serving with 52 Brigade, Royal Artillery, watched the attack from his observation post: 'As I watched the ranks of the Highlanders were thinned out and torn apart by an inaudible death that seemed to strike them from nowhere. It was peculiarly horrible to watch; the bright day, the little scudding clouds and these frightened men dying in clumps in a noiseless battle.'

The **third attack** on Roeux began on 23 April and XVII Corps was ordered to attack with two brigades of the 51st (Highland) Division. The 154 Brigade attacked south of the railway line and made some progress into the village with 4/Seaforth Highlanders capturing the Chemical Works with assistance from a tank, only to be driven out again by a determined counter-attack. By the end of the day British units were left in possession of the western edge of the village. On 28 April the **fourth attack** was made by units of the 34th and 37th divisions, which made little headway in the face of strong counter-attacks. The 11/Suffolks attempted to take the Chemical Works but suffered badly in the process whilst 10/Lincolns reported

433 casualties, many of whom lie in **Roux British Cemetery**. During the **fifth attack** on 3 May, 12 Brigade (4th Division) advanced just to the east of the Chemical Works but were pushed back once again by German counter-attacks and artillery fire. Eight days later the **sixth attack** began at 7.30am on 11 May preceded by a very heavy bombardment. This time the troops were ordered to avoid the Chemical Works but to attack the area around the railway station and the land to the north, whilst other units attacked the village itself. Early the following morning all the objectives to the north of the railway were taken, and the western half of the village had been occupied. During the day efforts were made to consolidate the ground and that night the Germans evacuated the eastern half of Roeux and the Chemical Works, allowing the line to move forward to the eastern half of the village. Yet, despite all this bloodshed, the Germans were not content to let matters rest. On 15 May they attacked Roeux in force and successfully re-occupied the whole of the Chemical Works together with the trenches and buildings to north and south of the railway line. Finally, after protracted fighting, the Chemical Works were once again taken on 16 May, this time by the men of 5/Gordon Highlanders. In a little over a month, five separate divisions had fought amongst the ruins of Roeux and nearly 8,000 men had been killed or wounded. Roeux was held by the British until the Germans re-entered the village at the end of March 1918. It was finally retaken by the 51st Division on 26 August 1918. We look at Roeux in more detail in **Route 3**.

Continue along the D33 Rue Eugène Dumont for 300m until you reach **Rue des Canadiens** on the right. Park your vehicle off the road to see the remains of an ivy-covered blockhouse on the right that once formed part of the Roeux German defences around the château. A little further on is **Rue Guy Lemaire**, where you will find the memorial to the 11/Suffolks and **Lance Sergeant Charles Stevens**. After returning to your vehicle, pass the French war memorial on the right, continuing along the road until you cross the River Scarpe. This road will take you to Monchy-le-Preux where you can park in the square outside the *Mairie*.

Monchy-le-Preux

Described as one of – if not the – most vital position on the whole of the Arras battlefield, the village, with its high and commanding position, was captured by IR 153 on 2 October 1914 as part of the

German Sixth Army assault on Arras and it was not until 11 April 1917 that it fell once again in to Allied hands. Undeterred by the failure to take Monchy on the opening day of the 1917 Arras offensive, plans were put in place for an attack on 11 April to be made by 111 Brigade, 37th Division, along with units of 3 Cavalry Brigade and C Battalion, 1 Tank Brigade. It was, recalled **Lieutenant Leonard Chamberlen**, the intelligence and signalling officer of 13/Rifle Brigade, extremely cold with snow on the ground: 'The brigade started in blobs but extended into waves as they passed the copse and dashed up into the village, splitting into small parties to deal with houses, cellars and strongpoints still held by the Huns.'

The two leading battalions of 111 Brigade moved through the village to secure the perimeter by 9.00am and shortly afterwards cavalry from 10/Royal Hussars, Essex Yeomanry and 3/Dragoon Guards arrived to provide additional support. The organization of the village defences appears to have been left to 8 Cavalry Brigade, which took the brunt of the subsequent artillery bombardment. With the Germans still in possession of the high ground to the east of the village, the series of British assaults between mid-April and 23 June 1917 resulted only in the capture of the forward slopes of Infantry Hill by 76 Brigade. The cavalry action and the attack by 88 Brigade east of the village on 14 April are dealt with in more detail in **Route 5**. The German Mars offensive saw the 15th (Scottish) Division retiring from Monchy on 22 March 1918 and it was not until 26 August 1918 that the village was recaptured by the Canadian 5/Mounted Rifles.

The Château

To the left of the *Mairie* in the main square is the entrance to the former château and grounds where the two cavalry regiments of 8 Brigade, 3rd Cavalry Division, established their forward posts. The château building itself was used as one of the two dressing stations established by 8 Brigade, the second in a building near the crucifix on Rue de Tilleul. **Lieutenant Colonel Phillip Hardwick** commanding 10/Royal Hussars was wounded and command of both regiments devolved to **Lieutenant Colonel Francis Whitmore**, who consolidated the positions on the northern and eastern outskirts of the village.

The Newfoundland Caribou Memorial

Erected in 1919, the memorial is the work of the English sculptor Basil Gotto and was erected on a British bunker constructed by 69/Field Company overlooking Infantry Hill where the two

The Newfoundland Caribou Memorial at Monchy.

battalions of 29th Division suffered such heavy losses on 14 April 1917. The caribou sculpture is one of five situated across France and Belgium and readers of our *A Visitor's Guide: The First Day of the Somme: Gommecourt to Maricourt* will be familiar with the one in Newfoundland Park at Beaumont Hamel. The bunker was not completed until the beginning of December 1917. A plaque at the base of the memorial provides the visitor with a brief account of 1/Newfoundland Regiment's part in the battle.

The Village War Memorial
This is situated in front of the church next to the caribou and depicts a grieving mother and child. If you walk round to the rear of the memorial, an inscription acknowledges the help given by the Isle of Wight in meeting the costs of the village reconstruction; funds which were provided in memory of the men from the island who died on the Arras battlefield.

The Essex Regiment and Essex Yeomanry Memorial
This memorial is outside the church. Unveiled on 21 May 2016 by Baron Petre, Lord Lieutenant of Essex, it commemorates the events of 11 April 1917 when the cavalrymen of 8 Brigade assisted in the

A post-war study of Lance Corporal Harold Mugford VC.

The memorial to the Essex units that fought at Monchy and during the Arras offensive.

capture of the village. During this action **Lance Corporal Harold Mugford** held back the advancing enemy singlehandedly and was awarded the Victoria Cross. The memorial also commemorates the attack towards Infantry Hill made by 1/Essex on 14 April and the role of the Essex regiment in the Arras offensive.

The 37th Division Memorial

The monument is the work of sculptor Lady Feodora Gleichen, the sister of Major General Lord Edward Gleichen, who commanded the division from April 1915 to October 1916. Unveiled in October 1921, the

The 37th Division Memorial at Monchy.

memorial consists of three infantrymen standing with their backs to each other on a plinth listing the division's units and battle honours. Situated a few minutes' walk from the church on Rue de Tilleul, it can be found at the far end of a wall enclosing the Château Florent – one of the two châteaux in Monchy.

The *Calvaire* on Rue de Tilleul

Follow the Rue de Tilleul to the right for another 370m to where you will see a tall *calvaire* standing on a stone plinth with a former blockhouse which has been incorporated into the building on the right. Whether this was the blockhouse where **Lieutenant Charles Rutherford** of 5/Mounted Rifles encountered a group of Germans on 26 August 1918 and bluffed them into thinking they were surrounded, remains unclear. However, he took forty-five prisoners and three machine guns before directing his men to attack another blockhouse where they captured another thirty-five of the enemy. He was awarded the Victoria Cross.

Lieutenant Charles Rutherford VC.

From the *Mairie* take the D33 towards Wancourt which is signposted Wancourt and Arras. Continue past the communal cemetery where a plaque has been erected to record the gift of the cemetery gates in 1928 by the Isle of Wight. Continue – up what was called Hussar Lane – to the la Bergère crossroads. Turn right to reach the entrance to Windmill British Cemetery, located approximately 100m on the right and hidden behind some large industrial buildings. Take care here as the road can be very busy and parking outside the cemetery can be a little hazardous.

Windmill British Cemetery

The 29th Division began this cemetery in May 1917 and buried a number of the casualties from the fighting of 23 April. At the conclusion of the 1917 Battle of Arras the British front line was just over a mile – more than 1.5km – further east along the D939, rendering the cemetery vulnerable to enemy shelling and machine-gun fire. However, it continued to be used up until the German offensive of 1918. After the ground was re-taken in August 1918, burial parties continued to use the cemetery until October 1918. The last four men to be buried here were all Canadians, the most senior being 24-year-old **Major James Young** (II.H.17). Enlisting at Valcartier, Quebec,

James Young had been married in Paris in September 1914, only three months before his death. Buried next to him is 33-year-old **Sapper John Cameron** (II.H.16) and nearby is **Lieutenant Robert McMillan** (II.J.1) of 26 Brigade, Canadian Field Artillery, from Cape Breton, Nova Scotia. All three men were killed on 13 October 1918. The fourth, 23-year-old **Gunner Ernest Amirault** (II.H.14), also from Nova Scotia, was killed five days earlier serving with the Canadian Light Trench Mortar Battery. In Plot II, Rows D and E are buried twenty-three officers and men of 1/King's Own Royal Lancasters who died on the Drocourt–Quéant Line at the beginning of September 1917. Today the cemetery contains 402 burials of which thirty-five are unidentified.

From the crossroads continue south along the D33 – Spear Lane on British maps – until you see the Tank Cemetery on the right. There is parking directly in front of the 50m grass approach path.

The Tank Cemetery
The ground on which the cemetery is located was taken by 10/Loyal North Lancashires on 11 April. Suffering heavy casualties from enfilade fire directed from the high ground at Monchy-le-Preux,

Tank Cemetery.

a tank came to their aid enabling some progress to be made. It is assumed that the cemetery was named Tank Cemetery after this action. Ten men from 10/Loyal North Lancashires are buried in Row A near the right-hand wall and are most probably casualties from that encounter. Along the left-hand wall is a large grave containing sixty-four men from 7/Queen's Own Cameron Highlanders from 44 Brigade, 15th (Scottish) Division. This is a mass grave in what was a battlefield trench and several of the headstones bear more than one name. Theirs is a story of tenacity and courage and as you stand by their graves, look across the road to the ground over which they advanced on 23 April 1917. The brigade was tasked with the capture of the Blue Line including the village of Guémappe, the outskirts of which you can see some 700m to the east. Whilst 8/Seaforths were to take the village, 7/Cameron Highlanders were to advance north of Guémappe to the Blue Line running from **Cavalry Farm** – another kilometre beyond the village – to the River Cojeul. Cavalry Farm no longer stands but, at the time, was immediately south of the D939. The 9/Black Watch was to follow on, leapfrogging through to the next objective. German fire from the strongly garrisoned village of Guémappe pushed the Cameron Highlanders to the left, opening up a gap between them and the Seaforths on their right. The advance was checked by heavy artillery and machine-gun fire until 7.30am when the Cameron Highlanders, with some of the Black Watch, worked their way around the north of the village, forcing the Germans to retire and allowing the Seaforths to capture it. The occupation was short-lived: that afternoon a counter-attack pushed the Seaforths out of Guémappe and the Cameron Highlanders back to a line just west of the village. The lost ground was recovered by 46 Brigade and on 26 April the Cameron Highlanders finally took **Cavalry Farm** before they were relieved during the night of 28 April. During the period 23 April to 28 April 7/Cameron Highlanders recorded 380 men killed, wounded or missing. The cemetery contains 219 burials, twenty-five of which are unidentified.

Leave the cemetery and continue for another 500m until you see a CWGC signpost on your left for Guémappe British Cemetery. You can turn off the road here and park.

Guémappe British Cemetery
Approached along a short grass path, the cemetery is a memorial to the sacrifice of 8/Seaforth Highlanders who attacked Guémappe on 23 April. Eighty-seven officers and men of that battalion now lie in Plots I and II along with twenty-two men of 9/Black Watch. Unusually, Plot I also contains seven officers killed on 23 April and buried in Row E, the most senior being 23-year-old **Captain Leonard Morrison** (I.E.9) from St Andrews. Earlier in the day he had distinguished himself when he and half a company of his men held an exposed position in **Hammer Trench**, north of Guémappe. Ordered to withdraw temporarily in order to reduce casualties, he led another assault on the trench in the early evening. Although he was killed during the attack, his mixed group of Seaforths, Cameron Highlanders and Black Watch carried the position and advanced beyond it. Before you leave, spend a few minutes by the grave of **Lance Corporal William Reid** (I.B.3), who was killed on 26 April. Serving with 9/Black Watch, he was already the recipient of the MM and was killed during a night attack near Cavalry Farm.

Return to your vehicle and turn left onto the D33 to Wancourt. At the intersection the village war memorial is on your right where a left turn onto Rue d'Alsace will take you to Wancourt British Cemetery. If you continue straight ahead from the cemetery uphill onto the Wancourt ridge (best accomplished on foot) the site of the **Wancourt Tower** – a former windmill – can be visited (see **Route 6**). The tower is no longer in existence but was situated on the right of the track in the field opposite la Voie du Moulin which leads down to Guémappe.

Wancourt
After heavy fighting Wancourt was captured on 12 April 1917 by the 50th Division, the Germans withdrawing to the ridge east of the village, which you can see behind the cemetery. The 6/Northumberland Fusiliers' war diary records that 'the front line ran fifty yards west of the Wancourt Tower, which was occupied by the enemy'. **Second Lieutenant Sidney Greenfield**, serving with the battalion, recalled it was a 'rather unsatisfactory' state of affairs:

To our left was the village of Guémappe with the remains of a tank nearby. We were astonished to learn this was the front line. A quite untenable position on the reverse slope with the remains of a tower [Wancourt Tower] just in front and no obvious enemy in sight … we also learnt the Germans were still holding out in the village of Guémappe and had machine guns enfilading [us].

The tower was taken on 14 April by a platoon from Greenfield's battalion led by **Second Lieutenant William Darlington**, who was wounded during the assault. Sidney Greenfield was sent back to report to Brigade HQ whilst the assault went in: 'Darlington's men rushed forward with fixed bayonets and the Germans ran for their lives. They took the tower and its environs and the only casualty was Mr Darlington himself … the next time I saw him again was as he lay on the stretcher being carried back to the dressing station.'

A period of deadlock followed during which, according to the 50th Division war diary, the tower fell down. The 50th Division's report of the tower falling down conflicts with an account by **Captain John Glubb** from 7/Field Company, Royal Engineers, who wrote that the tower was demolished by a group of his sappers. The 56th Division history records that it was blown up by the Germans during the night of the 14th! We shall probably never know the reality of the situation, but we do know that on 17 April, 7/Northumberland Fusiliers finally occupied the ruins of the building for the last time. On 23 April the offensive continued with Guémappe as the objective of the 15th Division attacking east from Wancourt towards Vis-en-Artois and 150 Brigade attacking towards Chérisy. Several determined German counter-attacks were made but, by the morning of 24 April, the British held Guémappe and the high ground overlooking Fontaine-lès-Croisilles. The village reverted to German control during the 1918 offensive and it was not until 26 August 1918 that the Canadian 27/Battalion captured the large German command bunker at Wancourt and pushed on up the hill to take the ruins of the Wancourt Tower. Two days later the Canadians captured Vis-en-Artois and the Rouvroy–Fresnes Line at Boiry-Notre-Dame.

Wancourt British Cemetery
When the 50th Division opened this burial ground towards the end of April 1917, they called it Cojeul Valley Cemetery or River Road Cemetery. After the German 1918 offensive Wancourt was recaptured by the Canadians in August 1918 and following the Armistice, graves were brought in from the surrounding battlefields. Today there are nearly 2,000 burials, of which a staggering 829 are unidentified. Many of those killed serving with the 50th Division are amongst this number. **Captain Wilfred Bunbury** (Sp. Mem. 72) was one of the few men

Wancourt British Cemetery.

listed in 6/Northumberland Fusiliers' casualty list who was identified and has a headstone in the cemetery. Listed on the CWGC database as serving with 4/Northumberland Fusiliers, he was attached to the 6th Battalion in March 1917. There are three other identified men from Bunbury's battalion buried together in Plot IV. **Privates J. Brinton** (IV.C.29) and 23-year-old **Andrew Murray** (IV.C.31) are buried either side of 21-year-old **Corporal William Turnbull** (IV.C.30). All three men were killed on 15 April 1917. Amongst the thirty-one identified officers and men of the East Yorkshires, eighteen were killed serving with 4/East Yorkshires in 150 Brigade. The remaining men were serving with 1/East Yorkshires, 21st Division. One of the more well-known officers was 32-year-old **Captain Cyril Easton** (Sp. Mem. 61) whose MC was gazetted in January 1917. He and **Second Lieutenants Harold Oughtred** (V.C.39) and **Charles Boyle** (I.B.4) were killed near the Wancourt Tower on 23 April as they advanced towards Kestrel Copse on the Chérisy road, during the 150 Brigade attack on the German line. Finally, spare a thought for the soldier poet 26-year-old **CSM William Littlejohn** (V.E.16), who was killed serving with 1/7 Middlesex on 10 April 1917.

Retrace your route back into Wancourt and, following signposts for Héninel, turn left at the church onto the D33. After 1.2km you will arrive at a staggered crossroads in Héninel.

Héninel

The village of Héninel was captured on 12 April 1917 by the 56th and 21st divisions in what the 2nd City of London regimental historian described as terrible weather conditions, 'there was snow, sleet and a biting wind; and the men had to stand in open trenches with no semblance of protection'.

The attack was launched at 5.15am with the London Rifle Brigade on the left and 1/2 Londons on the right. B Company of 1/2 Londons bombed up the Cojeul Switch, and working round the south of Hill 90 joined hands with the London Rifle Brigade who had enveloped the other flank. This successful enterprise resulted in the capture of ten of the enemy and the killing of many others. At 5.35am the enemy could be seen withdrawing from Héninel.

The history of the 56th Division records that it was found necessary to have a password during the operation so that converging parties did not bomb each other: 'To the great amusement of the men the words "Rum jar" were chosen. The Germans, being bombed from both sides, must have thought it an odd slogan.'

On your left is a profusion of CWGC signposts directing you to six cemeteries. Turn left to pass the *Mairie* on your immediate right, and continue past the church and village war memorial to bear left at the

The Mairie *at Héninel.*

fork ahead. Go past the entrance to **Héninel Communal Cemetery Extension** on your left (see **Route 6**) and bear right at the next fork from where you should be able to see the Cross of Sacrifice at Chérisy Road East Cemetery. However, beware as parking is tight outside the cemetery.

Chérisy Road East Cemetery

Cherisy Road East Cemetery was made by the 30th and 33rd Divisions' Burial Officers in April 1917 and all sixty-three identified burials are from April 1917; the nineteen unidentified burials were probably killed during April 1917 too. This is a battlefield cemetery where most, if not all, the casualties have been buried in one collective grave and the visitor will notice there is often more than one name on the headstones. The vast majority of the casualties are from the Liverpool and Manchester regiments of the 30th Division. **John Robertson** (Grave 42), aged 32, of 2/Royal Scots Fusiliers is listed as a private soldier in the CWGC records but elsewhere his rank is given as sergeant. Before enlisting in 1914 he had been employed in Glasgow by Messrs A.G. Barr at Parkhead. He was killed on 23 April 1917 during the battalion's attack on the Hindenburg Line.

> Return to the fork in the road and turn right, the triangular shaped Bootham Cemetery is 470m further on. There is plenty of parking here.

Bootham Cemetery

The cemetery derives its name from the nearby **Bootham Trench**, which in turn was named after Bootham School in York. It is really ill-named as it is almost on the site of **Egret Trench**, one of a series of trenches having an ornithological theme – 'Crow', 'Buzzard', 'Kestrel', 'The Nest' and 'The Rookery' amongst others . It was begun in April 1917 by the 56th Division's Burial Officer. This is another battlefield cemetery with the casualties buried together in one long trench – consisting of four plots – of which seventy-one of the 186 burials remain unidentified. Half the burials are officers and men of 2/Royal Scots Fusiliers, 33rd Division, who took part in the attack on the Hindenburg Line on 23 April 1917. Their casualties numbered more than 150 killed in the attack. **Private Francis Hendrick** (D.15), aged 19, also has his name on the family headstone in St Kentigern's Roman Catholic Cemetery, Maryhill, in Glasgow. Another 19-year-old in the same battalion and also from Glasgow was **Private James Lee** (C.11). The Queen's Westminster Rifles (1/16 Londons) are also represented here with forty-three casualties from the attack on Héninel on 14 April 1917. Of the 300 casualties the battalion sustained that day, twelve officers were killed or wounded.

Continue towards the line of wind turbines on the ridge ahead of you. Running across the road, 400m before the communal cemetery, was the British front line, which represented the limit of the British advance in May 1917. The German front line ran parallel to the British and ran through the northern tip of the cemetery. Bear left at the fork in the road and continue on the D38 into the village.

Chérisy
Cherisy was captured by the 18th Division on 3 May 1917, but lost the same night, remaining in German hands until it was taken by the Canadian Corps on 27 August 1918; the line of cemeteries east of the Sensée River representing the limit of the Canadian advance on 27 August 1918. On 2 May 1917, 55 Brigade was ordered to attack the northern end of the village and the two assaulting battalions of 54 Brigade were assigned to the southern end. Defended by the heavily wired **Fontaine Trench** and 'an orchard full of machine guns' the numerous sunken roads around the village aided its defence considerably. What might have assisted the British battalions in holding on to the village was the original first light start time but, for some inexplicable reason, the start was brought forward to the early hours. The darkness at 3.45am proved too much for the assaulting troops of 54 Brigade who lost touch with flanking units and, in the ensuing muddle, could get no further than **Fontaine Trench**. Some of 12/Middlesex managed to get into the village on the left and held a tenuous line along the river but seeing 55 Brigade falling back, followed suit. At the crossroads with the D9 you have the opportunity to turn left to the site of the statue of **St Michael**, which you will find 600m further along the road. The line between here and **Triangle Wood** to the northeast – **Michael's Road** on trench maps – represented the first objective of 41 Brigade, 14th Division, on 3 May and was effectively the limit of their advance. At the time of writing the statue of St Michael was absent and only the plinth remains.

Retrace your route to the crossroads, turning left on the D38 towards Hendecourt-lès-Cagnicourt, and follow signs for Sun Quarry Cemetery, passing over the Sensée River, which is very easy to miss! After 900m the cemetery appears on the left where there is parking.

Sun Quarry Cemetery

The cemetery takes its name from a flint quarry, known to the army as Sun Quarry, which was directly opposite the cemetery in the right angle made by the D38 and the narrow track leading down to Fontaine-lès-Croisilles. The cemetery was made by Canadian units in 1918 and most of the 191 casualties were killed between 26 August and 28 September during the successful advance in 1918. Whilst the majority of British casualties are gunners, there is one casualty from the fledgling RAF buried here. On 27 August 1918, two Sopwith Camels from 208 Squadron were shot down during low-level attacks on a desperate German defence of the area. Glasgow-born 20-year-old **Lieutenant Jack Mollison** (C.11) was last seen at 4,000ft with four enemy aircraft from *Jasta* 26 chasing him down near Vis-en-Artois. Mollison's brother, William, died of wounds on 1 October 1918 when he was serving with the Machine Gun Corps. As one might expect, the majority of burials are Canadians from the 2nd Canadian Division who were probably killed during the final days of August 1918 attacking Hendecourt-lès-Cagnicourt and the Drocourt–Quéant Line. One of these men was 27-year-old **Private Harold Payne** (D.2), who was serving with 2/Battalion. He was an Anglican minister after graduating in 1916 from Huron College and chose to enlist rather than preach. He was killed on 30 August 1918.

Leave the cemetery and continue along the narrow D38 to pass Hendecourt Communal Cemetery on the right.

Sun Quarry Cemetery.

The magnificent eleventh-century **Château d'Hendecourt** and much of the village was destroyed by shellfire during the artillery bombardment preceding the assault on Bullecourt on 3 May. The present building, on land between Rue du Mont and Rue de Cagnicourt, was completed in 1927.

> At the T-junction with the D956 turn right and after 130m turn left onto the D38, signposted Quéant and Riencourt-lès-Cagnicourt. After 1km you will reach a T-junction in the village of Riencourt where a right turn will take you to the *Mairie* on the left. Now, before you get to the church, take the next road on the right – then turn left again at the junction after 100m to follow Rue du Cornet for 157m where you can bear right onto Rue de Bullecourt.

Using this minor road – which was known as **Diagonal Road** – you will pass the former **Six Crossroads** east of Bullecourt – now four if you count the track running north – and, after 170m, the re-aligned start of **Central Road**, which you will see on your left further along the road. Much of the Australian action of 11 April and 3 May 1917 took place in this area.

Bullecourt Cross Memorial
The memorial is on the right-hand side of the road – now known as **Rue des Australiens** – but beware, there is very limited parking here, so if you are going to stop, ensure you draw your vehicle well off the road. At this point you are just behind what was the second line trench of the German Hindenburg system which became the new Allied front line – **Joy Ride** – when the Germans eventually gave ground on 17 May 1917 after the second battle. If you turn with your back the memorial, the front line trenches of the **Hindenburg Line** ran almost parallel with this road some 200m directly in front of you, with the British and Australian front line immediately beyond. The roll of honour can be found in the green box fixed to a tree. The memorial was erected in 1982 after an idea first formulated by André Coilliot and the Australian historian John Laffin. In the fields opposite the memorial was where **Lieutenant Rupert Moon**, serving with the Australian 58/Battalion, earned the Victoria Cross on 12 May.

The Bullecourt Memorial Park
After a further 400m is the Memorial Park which was opened in April 1992 by Ben Humphreys, the Australian Minister for Veterans'

The Missing in Action Memorial at Bullecourt.

The memorial is almost entirely covered with plaques.

Affairs. A year later the bronze statue of the Australian soldier was unveiled on Anzac Day, 25 April 1993, exactly a year after the park was first opened. Designed and created by Peter Corlett, the statue is a replica of his own father, **Private Kenneth Corlett**, who fought at Bullecourt with 4/Australian Field Ambulance. Each year, on the nearest Saturday to Anzac Day on 25 April, ceremonies take place here and in the village. There is plenty of parking outside the park where a Ross Bastiaan sculpture of the battlefield and two information boards provide the visitor with a brief outline of the 1917 battles.

Peter Corlett's statue at the Memorial Park is a replica of his own father, Private Kenneth Corlett.

Continue towards the village, bearing left at the junction to arrive at the church and village war memorial. **Route 7** begins from here and there is plenty of parking opposite the *Marie*.

The Battles of Bullecourt

The First Battle of Bullecourt was originally scheduled to take place on 10 April 1917 with the support of a dozen tanks but the failure of the tanks from D Battalion, 1 Tank Brigade, to arrive on time led to the cancellation of the operation amidst a flurry of snowfall and driving sleet. The fact that the message to abort the attack did not reach two battalions from the British 62nd (West Riding) Division, which led to them suffering 162 casualties in the process of retiring, was a bad omen for the following day. On 11 May, despite Australian objections, the 62nd Division was ordered to attack the village frontally and from the west whilst the 4th Australian Division was tasked with attacking the village's eastern flank. Eleven tanks arrived on the start line but only one actually made it into Bullecourt. In spite of this failure the Australian infantry advanced northwards and seized two lines of German trenches in the Hindenburg Line.

Eventually, the Australians were driven back to their start line by a German counter-attack with the loss of over 3,000 men, more than a third of whom were taken prisoner. With the failure of the Australian assault the 62nd Division attack did not take place.

The **Second Battle of Bullecourt** began on 3 May 1917 and involved the 2nd Australian Division and the 62nd Division, which this time deployed all three of its brigades to attack simultaneously. They were supported by eight tanks from D Company, 1 Tank Brigade, three of which got into the village. This time the attack was preceded by a heavy artillery bombardment with the main Australian attack capturing the same trenches the 4th Australian Division had been ejected from on 11 April. A party of 2/5 West Yorkshires from 185 Brigade entered the village and held out in the church before they were pushed out by Germans and on the north side a group of men from 2/7 Duke of Wellington's and 2/8 West Yorkshires from 186 and 185 brigades reached the sugar factory before being surrounded and cut off. The Germans finally gave ground on 17 May and the new front line – Joy Ride Trench at the Bullecourt Cross memorial where you were earlier – remained in place until March 1918. Of 150,000 men from both sides who fought at Second Bullecourt, some 18,000

The Slouch Hat Memorial.

British and Australians and 11,000 Germans were killed or wounded in battle.

The Slouch Hat Memorial – backed by flagpoles – is situated in front of the church and commemorates the Australian and British soldiers who fell in the area during the two battles of Bullecourt. Next to it you will find the Memorial to D Battalion, 1 Tank Brigade: the section of tank track is from tank No. 586, which was commanded by 24-year-old **Second Lieutenant Harold Clarkson** and was destroyed, killing its commander, between Bullecourt and Riencourt on 11 April 1917. Harold Clarkson is commemorated on the Arras Memorial. Whilst you are here it is worthwhile heading south on the D956 and taking the second right on to the Rue d'Arras to visit the **Bullecourt Museum** which was opened in 2012 and is based on the life's work of Bullecourt residents the late Jean and Denise Letaille. There is a Facebook page – *Friends of the Bullecourt Museum* – devoted to the museum which has a large collection of artefacts from the Hindenburg Line and the battles around Bullecourt. Entrance is €3 and it is well worth a visit.

From the museum on Rue d'Arras, continue to the *calvaire* and stop. The mound on which the *calvaire* is situated formed the western edge of the area known as the **Red Patch** which was a small salient

The Memorial to the tanks of D Battalion at Bullecourt.

defended by the German Guards Fusiliers. Rue d'Arras formed the centre line of the Red Patch, and the failure of 2/5 West Yorkshires to surround the salient on 12 May, preventing German reserves from reinforcing the Red Patch from the main Hindenburg Line defences, prolonged an already bloody battle, which was not concluded until dawn on 17 May.

> From the *calvaire* continue on Rue d'Arras as the road bends sharp left towards Écoust-St-Mein. Drive slowly as you enter the village as the entrance to Écoust Military Cemetery is only a few metres after the junction on the right, signposted *Déchetterie* (rubbish tip). The pathway to the entrance is on the right and marked by a set of three steps between two houses. Access to this beautiful cemetery is along a grass pathway which runs beside the former Boisleux–Marquion railway embankment. This is the same old railway that features in **Route 7** at Bullecourt and which ran to the west of the village providing the jumping off line for the Australians. Parking here is difficult and it may be sensible to park off the road on the track which is almost opposite the cemetery pathway.

Écoust Military Cemetery

Écoust-St-Mein was captured by 8/ and 9/Devons, 7th Division, in a blizzard on 2 April 1917 and lost again during the German offensive on 21 March 1918. The village was retaken at the end of the following August by the 3rd Division. The cemetery was begun in April 1917 and used until March 1918. A number of burials were then made by the Germans and, after the Armistice, further graves, almost all of 2/6 North Staffords, were brought into Plot II from a position just outside the cemetery. Today the cemetery contains 156 burials, half of which are unidentified. There are also seventy-one German burials here from March 1918, many of which are unidentified. The most senior casualty here is 44-year-old **Lieutenant Colonel Thomas Thorne** (II.B.20), who was commanding 2/6 North Staffords on 21 March 1918 when he was killed during the Battle of Bapaume. He lies in the same row as the men of his battalion who were all killed on the opening day of the German offensive. Also well represented are men of the 62nd (West Riding) Division who died during the assaults on Bullecourt. Before you leave take a moment to ponder over the grave of 22-year-old **Private William Camplin** (I.B.15) from Church Street in Barnsley, who was serving with 2/5 York and Lancaster Regiment when he was killed on 21 May 1917.

Écoust Military Cemetery.

> Continue to the roundabout. Should you wish to visit the grave of the poet
> and writer **Captain Arthur West** in the HAC Cemetery, continue straight
> ahead for another 1.3km on the D956, but our route does not include this
> cemetery as we are turning right to follow signs for Écoust-St-Mein British
> Cemetery, which is a short distance along the road on the right.

Écoust-St-Mein British Cemetery

What immediately strikes the visitor on entering this cemetery –
which was a continuation of a German Extension (now removed) of
the communal cemetery – are the graves of fifty officers and men of
13/King's Liverpool Regiment who were casualties of the battalion's
attack on Écoust on 30 August 1918. The war diary reported nine
officers and 200 other ranks killed, wounded or missing. They held
the village until 2 September when 8 Brigade passed through them as
part of the general attack on Lagnicourt by the 3rd Division. One of
these men was 20-year-old **Second Lieutenant Phillip Hillier** (D.14),
whose commission had been gazetted just two months previously
on 28 May 1918. Another large group of casualties is from 1/Royal
Scots Fusiliers who were heavily engaged on 2 and 3 September at

Noreuil, losing six officers and forty-three other ranks killed with a further nine officers and 137 other ranks wounded. **Lieutenant John Charlton** (D.3), aged 26, was killed on 2 September along with twelve men who can be found in rows A and D. One of the six Canadian soldiers buried here is 19-year-old **Private Rocky Karst Jordan** (B.26), 47/Battalion, who was born in Naples, Italy and lived in Cooper Street, Jackson, Michigan, USA before the war. Jordan enlisted in London, Ontario on 17 February 1918 and arrived in France on 20 August. During operations for assembly of troops prior to an attack on the Marquion Line a shell burst near his trench on 26 September and he was wounded in the left arm, thigh, both legs and foot. He died of his wounds at the 3/2 West Lancashire Field Ambulance.

Leave the British Cemetery and, after passing the communal cemetery, continue uphill on the D5. If you look across to your right you will see the line of trees marking the former 26km-long Boisleux–Marquion railway line – nicknamed 'the yo-yo' – which was in operation between 1882 and 1969, apart from the war years. The railway crossed the road at the point where the trees converge with it up ahead. Continue towards Croisilles.

Croisilles
After a disastrous attempt to capture it on 28 March 1917, the village was finally taken on 2 April by 91 Brigade, 7th Division, whose orders were not to attack Croisilles directly but 'pinch it out' in conjunction with the 21st Division. The 2/Queen's Royal West Surreys began their attack at 5.15am and almost immediately were straddled by their own barrage; the leading company losing all its officers. Nevertheless, after reorganization, the attack continued but was delayed again by a heavily defended position along the railway embankment known as **The Tooth**. Here the embankment was some 40ft high and sustained machine-gun and sniper fire caused heavy casualties amongst the Queen's before they arrived at their first objective north of the railway line. Unfortunately, as the 7th Division historian was at pains to point out, the 21st Division failed to arrive on time and many of the German defenders managed to escape back to the **Hindenburg Line**. Undeterred by this hiccup in the operation, the village was finally taken and two companies of 22/Manchesters cleared the village with a further loss of five officers and thirty-nine men. The village was in British hands by 2.00pm. The village fell again on 21 March 1918 during the German offensive and proved to

be difficult to reoccupy in August 1918. The 1 Guards Brigade had already been thrown back during their attack on the right flank of the village and the assault by 2/Londons, 56th Division, on 28 August was once again met with heavy machine-gun fire. This weight of fire pinned the attacking troops down and it was only with the use of trench mortars that progress was made. **Lieutenant Colonel John Kellett**, commanding the battalion, remarked that the enemy 'were mostly young men, who fought stubbornly, and were dislodged only with the greatest difficulty'.

Once you have arrived on the outskirts of Croisilles head towards the church and, at the intersection, turn left along Rue St-Leger – signposted 'D5, St-Leger, Achiet le Grand'. You should also see a green CWGC signpost for Croisilles British Cemetery. After 300m turn left along Rue Eugène Hornez to find the cemetery on the right, where there is plenty of parking near the former railway line. If you walk on a little further you will come to the junction of two tracks. This is the site of **The Tooth** that caused so much difficulty to 2/Queen's in April 1917.

Croisilles British Cemetery

One thing that strikes the visitor to this cemetery is the high cost in casualties of localized actions and the determination of the defending garrison to sell their positions dearly. Plots I and II were made between April 1917 and March 1918 and the rest were formed after the Armistice when graves were brought in from the neighbouring battlefields. The majority of the 1,171 soldiers buried in the cemetery belong to the Guards, 7th and 21st divisions and of these 647 are unidentified. The cemetery also contains the graves of six airmen of the Second World War and eighteen German war graves. There are a large number of men who were killed during the 1917 and 1918 attacks on the village and surrounding area, amongst them are the twenty-two identified men of 22/Manchesters who were all killed on 28 March 1917 during the first attack on Croisilles, which ended in disaster for the battalion. Thirty-five of the identified 2/Queen's were killed during the second attack on the village on 2 April 1917, including 29-year-old **Lieutenant Frank Woods** (I.A.3) from Camberley, who joined the regiment in 1915, and Chiswick-born 22-year-old **Second Lieutenant Alfred Fitch** (I.A.2), who began his army service as a private in the Honourable Artillery Company before being commissioned into the Queen's.

There are a number of 16th (Irish) Division casualties from the November 1917 Hindenburg Line action around **Tunnel Trench**, which ran from Fontaine-lès-Croisilles towards Bullecourt. Before its eventual capture in November 1917, Tunnel Trench was subject to an attack by 2/Royal Welsh Fusiliers in May and eleven men from that battalion lie scattered around the cemetery. One of these men, **Second Lieutenant Thomas Conning** (IV.B.3), was a friend of the poet Siegfried Sassoon and is mentioned by name in *The War the Infantry Knew* by Captain James Dunn, the battalion medical officer. Conning was killed on 27 May 1917 during an attack on the trench in which the battalion recorded losses of 165 officers and men. There are also fifty casualties from the 110 (Leicester) Brigade, the majority of whom were involved in the attack on **Tunnel Trench** in June 1917.

Before you leave find a moment to visit the crew of a Lancaster of 514 Squadron, which took off from Waterbeach, Cambridgeshire on the night of 16 June 1944 and was shot down over Croisilles. The only crew member to survive was the navigator, **Flying Officer Arnold Morrison**, who evaded capture and returned to England in September that year.

> Leave the cemetery and retrace your route back along the D9 to the main intersection in the centre of the village near the church. Turn left to take the D5 – Arras, Beaurains – to pass beneath the A1 Autoroute and railway line towards Hénin-sur-Cojeul. On entering the village pass the church on the left and continue over the crossroads for 230m to find Hénin Crucifix Cemetery on the right where there is parking.

Hénin-sur-Cojeul

The village was captured on 2 April 1917 by two battalions from 21 Brigade, 30th Division. It was one of several included in that day's operations to clear a line of outposts in front of the Hindenburg Line. As with Croisilles, the aim was for 2/Yorkshire Regiment and 19/Manchesters to pinch out the village and, after sealing the exits, clear the village of Germans. The battle, which raged all morning and into the afternoon, finally ended after the *Mairie* was captured at 3.00pm. The rebuilt *Mairie* can be seen near the church on Rue de Boiry. The village was lost again in March 1918 after an obstinate resistance by the 40th Division, remaining in German hands until the following 24 August, when it was liberated by the 52nd (Lowland) Division.

Hénin Crucifix Cemetery

This is a small cemetery – which takes its name from the *calvaire* that stands opposite the entrance – made by units of the 30th Division after the capture of the village in 1917.

Today there are sixty-one casualties buried here, two of whom are unidentified. The casualties include men killed in the attack on the village by the 30th Division on 2 April 1917 and a large number of officers and men from 20/King's Liverpool Regiment who were killed a week later on the opening day of the Arras offensive. **Second Lieutenant Alfred Carr** (A.39), aged 29, is almost halfway along the single line of headstones in the cemetery. A former pupil of Buxton College, he was employed as an actuary in Manchester before joining the Royal Naval Division as an ordinary seaman in February 1915 and serving as a motorcyclist on the staff of 1 Royal Naval Brigade HQ. He served in Gallipoli and was mentioned in dispatches in November 1915 before he was discharged to a commission in December 1916. He was one of two officers from 17/Battalion King's Liverpool Regiment – not 9/Battalion as listed – who were killed on 9 April.

After leaving the cemetery you have a choice of routes, depending on the vehicle you are driving. The most direct route is to continue along the D5 for 130m to a crossroads where a right turn along an unmetalled track for 700m will take you to a crossroads marked by a shrine on the left. Turn left and continue along the narrow road until you see Neuville-Vitasse Road Cemetery on the left. The other choice is to retrace your route and at the first crossroads, turn left onto **Rue Guislain Debeugny** and follow the road round a sharp left-hand bend to reach the shrine. Go straight on to find Neuville-Vitasse Road Cemetery.

Neuville-Vitasse Road Cemetery

This is another small cemetery which has eighty-six burials of which eleven are unidentified. Almost all the casualties here are from the opening day of the Arras offensive. Given the proximity of the 1/7 Middlesex action in the Hindenburg Line on 9/10 April 1917, it is strange that only one man from the battalion is buried here. **Private Gilbert Cox** (C.9), aged 25, from Ilchester in Somerset, most probably died of wounds on 11 April 1917. The 30th Division was operating on the right flank of the 56th Division – 21 Brigade's advance began at 11.30am – and although they crossed this road they encountered the heavily wired and defended **Neuville-Vitasse Trench**, which was about 400m east of the cemetery. The 2/Wiltshires' casualties in particular – fighting across this very ground that day – were very heavy with the war diary listing 342 officers and men killed, wounded or missing. Two men of the same age were amongst the Wiltshires' dead: 20-year-old **Private Reginald Skull** (B.10) was already the holder of the MM and was posthumously awarded the DCM for his work as a runner and **Second Lieutenant Stanley Horton** (B.2), who enlisted in 1914 into the Public Schools Battalion before he was commissioned. The youngest is probably 18-year-old **Lance Corporal Bernard Jeans** (C.23), who was one of five brothers and sisters living in Stourton, Wiltshire. Mercifully, his two younger brothers were not old enough to enlist before the Armistice was declared.

Leave the cemetery and continue towards Neuville-Vitasse. By the end of the day's fighting on 9 April 1917 the British had dug in along the line of this very road. Stop after about 600m and look some 200m into the fields on the right to where the first-line trench of the Hindenburg Line – **Neuville-Vitasse Trench** – ran northwest–southeast. Running at right angles to it opposite this spot was **Lion Lane**, where **Lieutenant Colonel Stanley King**'s men and the 1/Londons finally broke through the line. Continue into Neuville-Vitasse and after following the D34 through the village stop outside the church and village war memorial on the left.

Neuville-Vitasse

There is little doubt that the position and design of the Hindenburg Line made the attacks south of Neuville-Vitasse a far more difficult task for the British divisions. The attack on Neuville-Vitasse was allotted to 167 Brigade, 56th Division, whose objective was the Blue Line, which ran roughly round the eastern exits of the village from the sugar factory in the south – the site of which is on the east of the D5, about 600m from the crossroads with the D34 – to a point where the railway crossed the Hindenburg Line, often referred to as the **Cojeul Switch Line** – to the northeast. Lieutenant Colonel Stanley King established his 1/7 Middlesex Battalion HQ in the ruined sugar factory at about 1.00pm on 9 April 1917. The village was a strongly defended outpost of the Hindenburg Line and in front of the snout of the main trench – **Neuville Work or Redoubt** – was **Neuville Mill**, a concrete blockhouse built underneath an old windmill and designed to bring fire to bear on any frontal or flanking attacks. The site of this blockhouse can still be seen about 600m along the

D34 Neuville-Vitasse to Mercatel road, marked by a patch of waste ground and scrub. The 3/Londons cleared this position with the aid of a tank which fired directly through the machine-gun aperture. The 167 Brigade continued through the village with 1/8 Middlesex taking the church, where they were temporarily held up by a machine-gun post. Attention now moved to the east of the village where 1/Londons had failed to break through the Hindenburg Line. Carrying the Londons with them, Lieutenant Colonel King's men managed to take Telegraph Hill Trench but it was not until 3.00am on 10 April that the Hindenburg Line was finally breached, leaving the way clear for offensive action to begin on the right flank. The village was almost entirely lost in March 1918 and recovered the following August.

The rebuilt church at Neuville-Vitasse.

Neuville-Vitasse church was the scene of the 1/8 Middlesex attack after they had forced their way into the village. Jonathan Nicholls, in his *Cheerful Sacrifice*, described the last moments of the German stronghold:

> When they reached the site of the destroyed church they found a strong pocket of Germans who had emerged from deep caverns into a final redoubt of sandbags, well protected with rolls of wire. They were the survivors of 163 Infantry Regiment and were determined to sell their lives dearly. They were soon surrounded and mercilessly showered with bombs. Just before 11.00am sixty-eight survivors, with four machine guns from this redoubt, surrendered. Neuville-Vitasse was in British hands.

The German account in the Regimental History of IR 163 details the attack on the village and that of the church:

> The enemy continued the assault against Neuville-Vitasse with battalions in four waves. The fight with the 11th *Kompanie* of *Leutnant* Jenz lasted ten minutes or so; explosions of hand

grenades and infantry firing could be heard. Hard hand-to-hand fighting commenced. Ten minutes and then *Leutnant* Jenz with his men were defeated. Outflanked on all sides they fought their last desperate fight in the remains of Neuville.

Leave the church and carry on to the crossroads. If you were to bear left along the D5, a short detour of some 600m would take you to the site of the former sugar factory on the left of the road, whilst another going straight across, again for some 600m, would take you to the site of Neuville Mill on the left of the D34. We are going to turn right, however, back onto the D5 towards Beaurains which will lead us to London Cemetery a little further along on the left.

London Cemetery
There are 747 casualties buried here, of whom 318 are unidentified. Commemorated separately on a wall at the far end of the cemetery are men who were formally buried elsewhere and whose graves were destroyed by shellfire. The 56th (London) Division attacked Neuville-Vitasse on 7 April 1917, two days before the main offensive was launched, when 1/Londons attempted unsuccessfully to

London Road Cemetery.

eliminate **Neuville Mill**. Seven of the men killed in this attack are commemorated on the surrounding panels and two have headstones, one of these was **Private John Hill** (I.B.3) from Roscoe Street, London, who was 33 years old and serving in A Company when he was killed. There are a number of men commemorated or buried here from 3/Londons who took Neuville Mill and 1/8 Middlesex who cleared Neuville-Vitasse and the area around the church. Two 23-year-old subalterns, both commissioned in December 1915, were amongst the dead of A Company, 1/8 Middlesex: **Second Lieutenant Reginald Attwater** (Panel 4) was commissioned from the ranks, as was **Second Lieutenant Charles Askew** (Panel 2). It is highly likely that both boys served together in the ranks before being commissioned. In Plot I, Row A, are fifty-nine casualties from 12/Londons who were killed on 9 April and are buried together in a former trench. Two of these men are 20-year-old **Second Lieutenant Percy Peebles** (I.A.3) from Norwich, who was commissioned in July 1916. He spent less than eight months in France before his death. Killed in the same attack was Wiltshire-born 27-year-old **Second Lieutenant Edmund Hibbard** (I.A.4), who was commissioned from the Rifle Brigade in October 1916. **Second Lieutenant Charles Littlewood** (Wancourt Road Cemetery No. 2 Memorial, Panel 1) was the 19-year-old Royal Engineer who was responsible for the demolition of the Wancourt Tower (see **Route 6**). A former pupil of Downside School, he was killed during the night of 10 July 1917 near Kestrel Copse. His MC, awarded for 'conspicuous gallantry and devotion to duty [in carrying] out the strengthening of a brick bridge under hostile barrage. His coolness and example enabled the work to be completed without cessation, despite casualties', was notified in a second supplement to the *London Gazette* just eight days after his death.

Eight identified men of the Canadian 24/Battalion lie in Plot 2, all victims of the fighting of 11 April 1918 at Neuville-Vitasse when German infantry attempted to take the Canadian trenches. Initially successful, the Canadians counter-attacked and drove the enemy back to their start point. Seventeen Canadians were killed and another forty wounded. American-born **Private Alfred Johnston** (II.D.11) was 23 years old when he died and not 18 as stated in CWGC records; he died alongside former Scots Guardsman **Sergeant Robert Kydd** (II.B.30), who emigrated to Canada after being discharged. He is also commemorated on the family headstone in St Vigeans Old Churchyard, Arbroath. A reminder of the air war is 19-year-old **Second Lieutenant Sidney Stanley** (II.G.15) who was the pilot of a Bristol F2B from 11 Squadron on a photo reconnaissance flight.

He and his observer were shot down on 17 October 1917 over the Sensée Canal; both men were taken prisoner but Stanley died of wounds on 19 October. Another 11 Squadron pilot was 22-year-old **Lieutenant Alfred Speer** (I.C.1), who was shot down by anti-aircraft fire near Moyenneville, northeast of Bapaume, flying an FE2b on an offensive patrol on 9 July 1916. Casualty reports suggest that both Speer and his observer, **Second Lieutenant William Wedgwood**, had been burned in the wreckage. Initially buried by the Germans with nine more British soldiers in a small cemetery south of Courcelles-

Second Lieutenant Sidney Stanley.

le-Comte – just 100m or so from the small, present-day French military cemetery on the D32 – they now lie buried in the same grave. Speer qualified as a pilot at the Military School in Norwich in January 1916.

Appendix I

Where to Find the Victoria Cross Winners

Between 21 May 1916 and 26 December 1918 thirty-two men were awarded the Victoria Cross for gallantry in the field in the region covered by this guide. Of these, five were awarded for actions on 9 April, the opening day of the Battle of Arras. Thirteen awards were made posthumously and the recipients are buried or commemorated within the Arras area.

Name	Date of Death	Where	Reference
Jones, Lieutenant Richard *8/Loyal North Lancs*	21 May 1916	Broadmarsh Crater	Arras Memorial, Bay 7
Milne, Private William *16/Battalion CEF*	9 April 1917	Vimy Ridge	Vimy Memorial
Sifton, Lance Sergeant Ellis *18/Battalion CEF*	9 April 1917	Vimy Ridge	Lichfield Crater Panel 2, Column 2
Pattison, Private George *50/Battalion CEF*	10 April 1917	Vimy Ridge	La Chaudière Mil Cemetery (VI.C.14)
Waller, Private Horace *10/KOYLI*	10 April 1917	South of Héninel	Cojeul British Cemetery (C.55)
Mackintosh, Lieutenant Donald *2/Seaforth Highlanders*	11 April 1917	Fampoux	Brown's Copse Cemetery (II.C.49)
Cunningham, Corporal John *2/Leinsters*	12 April 1917	Bois en Hache	Barlin Communal Cemetery (I.A.39)

Name	Date of Death	Where	Reference
Hirsch, Captain David *4/Yorkshires*	23 April 1917	Wancourt	Arras Memorial, Bay 5
Harrison, Second Lieutenant John *11/East Yorkshires*	3 May 1917	Oppy	Arras Memorial, Bay 5
Jarratt, Corporal George *8/Royal Fusiliers*	3 May 1917	Pelves	Arras Memorial, Bay 3
White, Sergeant Albert *2/South Wales Borderers*	19 May 1917	Monchy-le-Preux	Arras Memorial, Bay 6
Cassidy, Second Lieutenant Bernard *2/Lancashire Fusiliers*	28 March 1918	St-Laurent-Blangy	Arras Memorial, Bay 5
Kaeble, Corporal Joseph *22/Battalion CEF*	8/9 June 1918	Neuville-Vitasse	Wanquetin Com Cemetery (II.A.8)
West, Lieutenant Colonel Richard *Tank Corps*	21 August and 2 September 1918	Croisilles	Mory Abbey Military Cemetery (III.G.4)

Appendix 2
Writers, Poets and Artists Killed at Arras

Men such as Isaac Rosenberg and Edward Thomas need little introduction and were well-known in their respective circles before the war. Others, such as Arthur West – who rose to prominence after the publication of *The Night Patrol* – and Robert Beckh, whose work was published posthumously in *Swallows in Storm and Sunlight*, were cut down before their writing was allowed to become established. Sadly, many more of the men in the list below fall under the heading of forgotten poets and writers of the First World War.

Date of Death	Name	Designation	Reference
30 April 1916	Pitt, Second Lieutenant Bernard *10/Border Regiment*	Poet	Arras Memorial, Bay 6
15 August 1916	Beckh, Second Lieutenant Robert *12/East Yorkshires*	Poet	Cabaret Rouge British (Marquilles Communal Cemetery German Ext 24)
3 April 1917	West, Captain Arthur *6/Ox & Bucks LI*	Poet/Writer	HAC Cemetery (VIII.C.14)
9 April 1917	Thomas, Second Lieutenant Edward *Royal Garrison Artillery*	Poet	Agny Military (C.43)
9 April 1917	Scanlan, Lieutenant William *5/Battalion CEF*	Poet	Barlin Communal Cemetery Ext (I.H.75)
9 April 1917	Wilkinson, Second Lieutenant Walter *1/8 Argyll & Sutherland Highlanders*	Poet	Highland Cemetery, Roclincourt (II.A.5)

Date of Death	Name	Designation	Reference
10 April 1917	Littlejohn, CSM William *1/7 Middlesex*	Poet	Wancourt British (V.E.16)
20 April 1917	Flower, Driver Clifford *Royal Field Artillery*	Poet	Arras Memorial, Bay 1
23 April 1917	Crombie, Captain John *4/Gordon Highlanders*	Poet	Duisans British (IV.A.22)
2 July 1917	Masefield, Captain Charles *1/5 North Staffords*	Poet/Writer	Cabaret Rouge British (VI.H.23)
23 March 1918	Wilson, Captain Theodore *10/Sherwood Foresters*	Poet/Writer	Arras Memorial, Bay 10
25 March 1918	Blackall, Lieutenant Colonel Charles *4/South Staffords*	Poet/Artist	Arras Memorial, Bay 2
1 April 1918	Rosenberg, Private Isaac *1/King's Own*	Poet/Artist	Bailleul Road East (V.C.12)

FURTHER READING

There is a veritable library of published titles covering aspects of Arras and limited space dictates that they cannot all be covered here. Three of the **Battleground Europe** titles published by **Pen & Sword** – www.pen-and-sword.co.uk – focus on the area covered by this guidebook and provide a host of supplementary information on some of the most visited parts of the area. Here you will find the personal experiences of soldiers, contemporary photographs and trench maps.

Bullecourt, Graham Keech
Monchy-le-Preux, Colin Fox
Walking Arras, Paul Reed

For battlefield visitors who wish to expand their knowledge with more in-depth reading, the following will be of interest:

McCrae's Battalion, Jack Alexander, Mainstream Publishing (2004)
Arras, Peter Barton and Jeremy Banning, Constable (2010)
Into Battle, John Glubb, Cassel (1978)
Cheerful Sacrifice, Jonathan Nicholls, Leo Cooper (1999)
VCs on the Western Front – 1917 to Third Ypres, Paul Oldfield, Pen & Sword (2017)
Armageddon's Walls – British Pill Boxes on the Western Front 1914–1918, Peter Oldham, Pen & Sword (2014)
Grandfather's Adventures in the Great War 1914–1918, Cecil Moorhouse Slack, Stockwell (1977)
A Life Apart, Alan Thomas, Gollancz (1968)
The Blood Tub, Jonathan Walker, Spellmount (1998)

INDEX